A Practical Guide to S[

Moving Beyond the Quality Time Myth

Quantity Time

By Steffen T. Kraehmer

DEACONESS PRESS
Minneapolis

Excerpt on page 4 by Eric Fellman in *Daily Guideposts* (April 13, 1988). Reprinted with permission from Daily Guideposts 1988. Copyright © 1987 Guideposts Associates, Inc., Carmel, NY 10512.

Excerpt on pages 13-14 by Linda Ching Sledge in *Daily Guideposts* (March 25, 1990). Reprinted with permission from *Daily Guideposts* 1990. Copyright © 1989 Guideposts Associates, Inc., Carmel, NY 10512.

Excerpt on page 16 from "Bill Cosby Himself." Reprinted with permission of the William Morris Agency, Beverly Hills, CA 90212.

"Cats in the Cradle" on pages 20-21 is by Harry Chapin. Copyright © 1974 Story Songs, Ltd.

Excerpt on page 26 from "Make Time for the Kids," the June 2, 1988, column by Ann Landers. Copyright © Ann Landers/Creative Syndicate 1988 and *The Times Herald Record*, Middletown, NY.

Excerpt on page 90 by Janet Martin in *Daily Guideposts* (June 13, 1981). Reprinted with permission from Daily Guideposts 1981. Copyright © 1980 Guideposts Associates, Inc., Carmel, NY 10512.

Excerpt on page 114 by Carol Knapp in *Daily Guideposts* (May 18, 1988). Reprinted with permission from *Daily Guideposts* 1988. Copyright © 1987 Guideposts Associates, Inc., Carmel, NY 10512.

Excerpt on page 145 from *The Power of Positive Students* by Dr. William Mitchell, with Dr. Charles Paul Conn. Copyright © 1985 by H. William Mitchell. Reprinted by permission of William Morrow & Co.

Excerpt on page 156 from *The Living Bible*. Copyright © 1971 owned by assignment by Illinois Regional Bank, N. A. (as trustee). Used by permission of Tyndale House Publishers, Inc., Wheaton, IL 60189. All rights reserved.

Excerpt on pages 160-61 from "Fragile Moments" by B. J. Connor in *Guideposts* magazine (March 1988). Reprinted with permission from *Guideposts* magazine. Copyright © 1988 Guideposts Associates, Inc., Carmel, NY 10512.

Excerpt on pages 167-68 entitled "To a Loving Parent" by Rita Shaw. Copyright © 1988 by Great Days Publishing Incorporated, Santa Barbara, CA.

Library of Congress Cataloging-in-Publication Data
Kraehmer, Steffen T.

      Quantity time: moving beyond the quality time myth/by Steffen T. Kraehmer.

            p.   cm.

      Rev. ed. of : Time well spent. © 1990

      Includes index

      ISBN 0-925190-30-6

      1. Parent and child—United States.   2. Parents—United States—Time management.

      I. Kraehmer, Steffen T. Time well Spent   II. Title

      HQ755.85.K73   1994   94-21343

      306.874—dc20   CIP

Published by Deaconess Press (2450 Riverside Avenue South, Minneapolis, MN 55454)

Cover/interior design by the Nancekivell Group
First Printing: July 1994
Printed in the United States of America.

97 96 95 94 7 6 5 4 3 2 1

Publisher's Note: Deaconess Press publishes books and other materials related to the subjects of physical health, mental health, and chemical dependency. Its publications, including *Quantity Time*, do not necessarily reflect the philosophy of Fairview Hospital and Healthcare Services or their treatment programs. For a current catalog of Deaconess Press titles, please call toll-free, 1-800-544-8207

Acknowledgements

I would like to express my deep gratitude to all the people who gave of themselves and one of life's most precious resources, their time, to make this book possible.

Susan Anderson	Phil Arnold
Jo Beecham	Diane Corritone Kramer
Linda Heitmann	Mary Lynn
Frank Machera, Jr.	Nance Muscatello
Inga Pellegrino	

Special thanks to Marianne Brosseau for her continuous support, editing skills, research, and guidance. Truly, this book would not have been completed without her ongoing assistance and belief in me and the information presented. I also appreciate Wendy Kondor assisting me in preparing this manuscript for it's second publication.

I'm also grateful to Jay Johnson and Ed Wedman for their professional assistance and interest in presenting this important message to parents in book form.

Author's Note: For convenience I have used the singular noun child throughout the book. However, experiences and suggested activities can be shared with more than one child.

In addition, I have used the noun parent. This reference is used as an umbrella term for parents, whether single or married, stepparents, or guardians. Although parent is used in the singular, I urge both parents to participate, if the family is a two-parent family. And, of course, grandparents, teachers, coaches or child-care workers - essentially any adult who is involved with a child on a regular basis - will benefit from the guidelines and recommendations in the pages that follow.

The names of some individuals in this book have been changed to ensure anonymity.

To my mother, Ingeborg Kraehmer, my wife, Sue, and my two sons, Ryan and Zachary. May I always spend time and enjoy memories with these very important people in my life.

Contents

Introduction

My father passed away on May 28, 1987, at the age of 67. He suffered from a prolonged series of ailments, including heart disease and diabetes and its complications. During my father's three-month stay in St. Francis Hospital, Poughkeepsie, New York, I found myself visiting him almost every day. During my hour-long drive to the hospital, I would think about my childhood and my father's involvement in it. My first six years, remembered mostly as a result of family discussions, included many good memories of family outings and togetherness times. When I entered school, I was spending more time with my three brothers and sister and friends, and less time with my parents. As adolescence approached, there was a distance between my father and me. My father was working seven days a week, sometimes by necessity and sometimes by choice. I can even recall some years that my father worked all 365 days, including Christmas.

Outside of work, my father started to develop leisure interests that took up most of his spare time. Having to work was one thing, but he chose to spend his leisure time away from his family. That was disheartening, and his absence left me with a void. It was a time in my life when I needed and wanted to be with my father. There was a desire within me that was difficult to comprehend and impossible to express, at least then. This need for closeness is something I wish my father had been aware of and had taken the initiative to fulfill during my growing-up years.

With my Dad now in the hospital, it was my turn to "make the time" available for him. I made the choice knowing that this might be the last opportunity to spend time with my father. The time together became very significant to me—and I hope to him, too. During some of my visits we had the opportunity to talk a great deal. Other times, I just sat in the room with him while he slept, being there for him if he woke up. I played the role of a care-giving parent, and he was a young child, roles which I was simultaneously experiencing as a first-time parent of an eighteen-month-old child.

While my father slept, I thought of the birth of my son, Ryan, and my father's lack of interest in that event. He also had the same lack of involvement when his other two grandchildren were born. Dad did not become absorbed in the excitement of his grandchildren, at least not outwardly. I had always hoped of developing a genuine attachment with my father, but that seemed elusive now that he was in the hospital.

On weekends my wife, Sue, and my son, Ryan, accompanied me to the hospital. At first we took Ryan with us to my father's room, but as Dad's health deteriorated, he did not seem to want a child around. During a "routine" weekend visit I went up alone to sit with my father. He inquired if Sue and Ryan were with me. I said, "Yes, they are waiting downstairs." He very excitedly asked if he could see Ryan. I was shocked and thrilled. Ryan came up to the room and my father seemed quite fond of my son. My father was sincerely reaching out to my son and to me. For me, it was a liberation of many years of suppressed feelings. The emotions we all expressed on that day are ones that I will cherish for a lifetime.

Finally I felt the closeness, the tie and the love that I had hoped for my son and his grandfather to share, even if it was only for a short time.

This book is all about the close relationship that can develop between a child and an adult. How to produce this bond comes down to two basic acts: the ability to express love and the willingness to share time together.

In today's fast-paced society, it is often difficult to "find the time" for your children. Spending time together and enjoying these togetherness opportunities create rewarding and lasting relationships, truly a significant accomplishment in anyone's lifetime. Fulfilling and long-lasting relationships between you and your child will not just happen. Relationships must be chosen, designed, and nurtured. Close relationships require an enthusiastic and loving attitude, a variety of activities and time set aside for them, and an abundant amount of open communication. The goal of this book is to help you realize the importance of spending quantity time with your child and to help you learn to establish opportunities for appreciating each other's company. To achieve that goal, each chapter contains guidelines for developing and strengthening your relationship with your child. I have called these principles "START," an acronym for Shaping Tomorrow's Adults by Reaching Out Today. When you initiate these principles and use them as a course of action, your relationship with your child will flourish.

The START principles will help raise your consciousness as a parent. Parents have one of the most difficult jobs in life, but parenting can also be one of the most rewarding life experiences. Parents have other obligations besides their children, and they have the need and desire to enjoy their own interests.

Over the years, I have organized, run, and evaluated youth programs for literally thousands of children, of all ages. I've found that parents who were genuinely interested in developing enriching relationships with their children would eagerly inquire about how to spend more time with their children. A common question was, "What do I do with my children?" This was usually followed by, "Now where can I find the time?" Essentially they where asking, "How do I begin to spend *more* time with my child?" The START principles, along with many time-saving techniques for maximizing your time at work and around the home (outlined in Chapter 3), will help you integrate all parts of your life and rearrange your priorities. Along with the START principles, Chapters 2-7 include activities called "Going the Extra Mile." These suggested activities provide you with an additional means for improving the parent-child relationship. "Going the Extra Mile" in whatever you do will give you that little extra. Trust that these activities will result in a greater return on the quantity time you invest in your child.

A child's upbringing is a complex, ongoing process. Providing quality education, health care, and day care are real concerns for the proper development of a child, and they all need to be addressed. Governments and educators must understand and better value the importance of our next generation. It is important for you to get involved on a local level with groups like the PTA, but remember, your meaningful role as a parent must come first. You are the most significant person in your child's life. you will build your child's future by raising him or her on a "one-to-one" basis.

When you raise or work with children, you are accomplishing more than just forming and molding a child. You are building tomorrow's adult and the world's future. Abraham Lincoln, the father of four boys, was a man with great insight, understanding and compassion for the United States and its citizens. He particularly realized the importance of our children:

"A child is a person who is going to carry on what you have started. . . . He is going to move in and take over your church, schools, universities and corporations. . . . The fate of humanity is in his hands."

You're the one who needs to reach out and find opportunities to enhance the growth of your child, your growth as a parent and, most importantly, your growth together as a family. START today!

How to Use This Book

Quantity Time and the START approach offer stepping-stones to an enriching relationship with your child. Everyday opportunities exist for you to do more, to be better, to become stronger, to understand more, or to live more fully as a parent. But you have to choose to accept the parenting challenge and travel the distance with your child. The result will be more than you can imagine.

There are many types of readers who will use this book. I have set up *Quantity Time* to accommodate different schedules and parenting needs. Select the method for using this book that best meets your situation:

1. Read the entire book in one sitting.
2. Read a chapter in one sitting.
3. Read one section at a time.

This book is conveniently divided into thirty-one sections for most of us busy parents who can't seem to "find the time" to read a book in one of the ways mentioned above. These thirty-one sections offer a daily reading, which coincides with the START principles. Begin by reading the introduction to Chapter 1, then read the START principle for DAY 1 and continue reading until you get to the next principle. (This will usually be about five or six pages.) Within thirty-one days you will have completed the entire book.

Quantity Time also offers you the option of using the thirty-one START principles in a monthly or yearly journal-style basis. Chapter 9 provides you with a monthly/yearly calendar of these START principles and a space for you to write down your application of them.

No matter how you read this book (and whenever you re-read this book), I know you will find time and time again a new awareness, a useful time-saving suggestion, a helpful parenting resource, or a much-needed bit of inspiration for your journey through life as a parent.

1

A New Life and Your Part in It

"Three essential elements for happiness are something to do, something to hope for and someone to love."

— *Dr. Joyce Brothers*

As millions of people watched television on October 14, 1987, more than 400 volunteers were racing against time to save an eighteen-month-old girl. Jessica McClure had fallen down an eight-inch-wide abandoned well pipe in the back yard of her aunt's home in Midland, Texas. At 7:55 P.M., October 16, feelings of helplessness and anxiety were replaced by feelings of joy and appreciation as Jessica was taken to the Midland Memorial Hospital for medical attention.

The world began to reflect on the past fifty-eight hours that Jessica had been trapped. Many lives were deeply touched by the successful rescue of this child. So many of us were reminded anew of how valued the life of one child is—to her parents, neighbors, relatives, teachers, and even to an entire nation.

A plaque was placed in Midland one year later to remember Jessica's triumph and honor those involved with this life-saving mission. The plaque reads, "Nothing the heart gives away is gone; it is kept in the hearts of others."

The date of Jessica's accident was significant to me because October 15, the second day of Jessica's traumatic experience, would have been my father's sixty-eighth birthday. And had he still been alive, he would have had a child Jessica's age in his life to care about, too—my son, Ryan. I reflected on the previous six months of life-changing events for our family and focused on the important role my wife and I now had in raising a child to become a healthy, happy, confident, and responsible individual. We knew that how we cared for him, what we did and said each day, was going to affect his happiness and well-being as he grew.

Every person who values a child, whether a parent or someone who works with children realizes that he or she is a "teacher" and will be an important influence on the child's life. This realization is the key motivating force that encourages an adult to continue fostering a child's learning and development in a positive manner. Adults who are committed to their child or to the lives of other children consistently recognize and experience the gratifying feelings that come from being devoted. This dedication demands that you sincerely believe that "a child is very important" and that all aspects of a child's upbringing—physical, mental, emotional, social and spiritual—are equally significant.

Besides providing a safe environment, how can we as adults in the role of parents fulfill all the necessary requirements of a maturing child? And how can we learn to appreciate all that we get from a child in return? Where do we start?

S T A R T IS: SHAPING TOMORROW'S ADULTS BY REACHING OUT TODAY

DAY 1 : START appreciating the beauty and remarkable development of your child. It stimulates a new and refreshing view of life and the world around us.

Ten Thousand Miracles a Day

More than 10,000 babies are born in the United States every day. Because birth occurs this many times a day, one tends to view it as an ordinary event. In fact, birth is one of the most extraordinary occurrences in the world. Hopefully each birth is perceived by the parents as a miracle, the beginnings of a new life, a human being who is a unification of two people. This birth offers the parents an extraordinary opportunity for a vibrant parenting experience and a strong parent-child relationship.

Consider the beginnings of each new life. Science tells us that when the twenty-three chromosomes of the sperm unite with the ovum's twenty-three chromosomes, a new forty-six-chromosome cell is formed. A mere four days after fertilization there is a tiny cluster of some sixty to seventy cells. The baby's heart starts beating from fourteen to twenty-eight days after conception (usually before the mother even knows she's pregnant), and by the thirtieth day almost every organ has started to form. During the first month of life, the embryo increases its size about forty-fold and its weight almost 3,000-fold. After one month, the heart beats 100,000 times each day. The embryo moves its arms and legs by six weeks and by forty-three days, brain waves can be read. Forty weeks of development will climax in the birth of a child. [1]

Once a child is expected, most parents naturally invest all their hopes in the child's staying healthy after a birth without incident. Such was the case with the parents of a newborn named Jenny, but she was born three months premature, weighing only two pounds and five ounces. She was immediately put on a respirator, taken to the Neonatal Intensive Care Unit, and placed in an isolette, which was to function as an artificial womb for the next few months. The first seventy-two hours of her life were critical and would not only determine if she would suffer any serious handicaps due to her prematurity, but whether she would survive her birth. Although she experienced one week of continuous weight loss and her weight was down to one pound and twelve ounces, her lungs started to function on their own, and she was removed from the respirator. Nine weeks after birth, Jenny was able to leave the hospital, weighing five pounds and two ounces. Why is this child so important to me? She is my brother's daughter.

Throughout Jenny's early weeks, her parents, family, family friends, and medical staff thought only of her survival. Through the wonders of scientific technology, the dedication and caring of a team of doctors and nurses and a tremendous amount of faith on the part of family and friends, Jenny survived and her prognosis was excellent. This core group of people realized the importance of saving a life and worked together to accomplish this mission. Once Jennifer was safe, I realized how focused I had been on her physical development, so much so that I almost forgot about Jenny the person.

As this dramatic case made clear, a child's health and safety are always a parent's first priority, but physical development is just one aspect of a child's growth. More difficult to measure, and sometimes more difficult to fulfill, are a child's emotional and psychological needs.

More Than Just Life's Basic Needs

Children need more than just food, clothing, shelter, and medical care. They need to feel secure and safe. This is demonstrated by a continuous desire for attention and assurance. A parent can fulfill these needs by the giving of themselves in the forms of time and love.

Eric Fellman, a father of three sons, shares the following story:

Our eight-year-old son Nathan is a lot like me, and it is sometimes difficult to see a carbon copy of myself walking around, making some of the same mistakes I did. In fact, because of this I've probably been harder on Nathan, our middle child, than on his two brothers.

The other night I was making the usual "drink of water, tuck in the blanket, give a kiss" rounds at bedtime. I came to Nathan last and was in a hurry to get back to reading the newspaper. Nathan looked up and asked, "Dad, can't you stay a little while?" I was about to tell him it was time to sleep, but something in his eyes stopped me. I stretched out beside him, and his arm went around my neck and his head onto my chest.

We talked about school and a few silly things. Finally I said, "Nathan, was there some reason you wanted me to stay?"

"No," he answered, "I just wanted to see if you would."

That hit me hard. What could be more important than spending time with a child who wanted to be with me? Not much, because all too soon he'll grow out of that need and I'll be asking *him* to spend a few minutes with his mother and me.[2]

All too often, children who look for love, security and a sense of direction, don't seem to find it in their families. Many are aimless and alienated, and alarming numbers of them have turned to drugs, alcohol, vandalism and violence.

As children grow, it is essential for them to feel wanted, secure, and especially loved.

Enriching Relationships

The movie industry has adopted the theme of spending time with a child and has produced such movies as *Mrs. Doubtfire*, *Baby Boom*, *Mr. Mom*, *Three Men and a Baby*, and its sequel, *Three Men and a Little Lady*. In each of the movies, the plot revolves around an adult or parent becoming involved with a child through some unique circumstance and the special relationship and bond that develops. Although these motion pictures are fiction, the message delivered—that spending time together enriches relationships—is quite accurate.

One of the all-time movie classics based on this theme is *Kramer vs. Kramer* (Studios, 1979). Joanna Kramer (Meryl Streep) leaves her husband, Ted (Dustin Hoffman), and her son, Billy (Justin Henry), on the evening that Ted finds out he is getting a promotion at work that he had worked very hard for. Along with coming to terms with his feelings, Ted Kramer realizes how drastically his work and home schedule will be affected by these changes. In one scene his lawyer explains the custody process, Ted's chances, and how much the legal battle will cost. He recommends that Ted make a list of the pros and cons of going through a custody fight. Later that evening, Ted sits alone in his living room making his list. In the pro column there is nothing listed as yet, while in the con column he has written money (lawyer's fees), no privacy, work, and no social life. He looks over the list, then goes into Billy's room and holds him saying, "I love you Billy. I know you're asleep and can't hear me, but I love you with all my heart." The decision is obvious; he elects to go to court. Ted's decision may not be pragmatic, but it's based on love. The movie shows how sometimes a difficult circumstance can enrich a relationship, but difficulty is *not* a prerequisite to developing enriching relationships. These can develop without distressing situations, if the parent takes the initiative.

Consistency and Stability

We all enjoy something that is reliable and lasting—a favorite movie, a restaurant that serves a special dish you love, a store that always carries clothes in your size. This feeling of contentment can also be found in relationships—a friend or relative who listens to you, a boss who compliments your work, a coach who gives you direction, a partner with whom you enjoy a certain activity and, of course, a child who counts on you. In order to develop a secure and eternal bond with an adult, a child needs to believe that a parent will always provide certain essentials whenever she or he needs them. What are these vital and basic requirements?

- A parent's expression of love and the continuous assurance that it will always be there.

- A parent's praise. All people, especially children, build greater confidence and a healthier self-image with positive reinforcement.

- Guidance tempered with understanding and clarification. Children appreciate knowing the reasons behind an action—not to rebel, but to understand. Although this is a time-consuming aspect of raising children, it builds trust and mutual respect when you "take the time" to explain.

- Clarification of a parent's values and morals. Getting through life is like traveling across unfamiliar country; directions are truly appreciated and beneficial. Values are usually learned and acquired through a parent's actions and lifestyle.

- Open lines of communication. Maintaining open communication involves an adult's time, genuine interest, and the ability to listen.

- Opportunities for the child to learn and grow physically, mentally, spiritually, emotionally, and socially. These opportunities are provided by the adult.

The child *and* the parent benefit when these principles are consistently followed. Emotional and psychological growth and maturity require close, positive, and caring relationships. A parent must strive for a relationship with a child that is built on love, trust, and patience.

DAY 2 : START being a major factor in building your child's personality, intelligence, and self-esteem. The sharing of your knowledge and love produces a strong foundation for your child.

A Strong Foundation

"If the foundation is secure, the structure will last forever" said a recent ad for a municipal bond insurance company in the *New York Times Magazine*. Structural foundations is one area where you should not try to skimp or short-change, as my wife and I found out.

In 1979, Sue and I moved back to New York from Connecticut with plans to build a house and "settle down." A relative had land we were going to buy, and he was planning to help us build a new home. The land was in the process of being subdivided and tested for a septic system. The process took much longer than we expected, and the final result was that the land did not meet specifications for proper drainage of a septic system. As could be expected, Sue and I were tremendously disappointed, having waited one year to hear the news. After finding another home that we are very pleased with, we realized that it all worked out for the best, despite the disappointment. Even if it had been feasible to build a foundation for a new house on that land, what would have happened in a year or two? The house may have shifted, or water problems could have caused structural and interior damage. Sue and I truly grasped the importance of a solid foundation for the safety and enjoyment of a home. Think about your child's foundation. What is it built upon? Is it on solid ground that will withstand years of service?

Dr. Benjamin S. Bloom, a Distinguished Professor of Education at the University of Chicago and past president of the American Educational Research Association, explains that a child's early environment is crucially important for three reasons. First, some of the most significant human characteristics (such as intelligence, academic achievement, generalized qualities of interest, and deep-seated personality traits) develop more rapidly in the first five years than they do over the remainder of a lifetime. The early environment shapes these characteristics in their most rapid periods of formation.

The early environment is also important, says Bloom, because of the sequential nature of much of human development. Each characteristic is built on a base of that same characteristic at an earlier time or on the base of other characteristics which precede it in development. Professor Bloom notes studies by a number of respected educators that support this observation: Erickson (1950) has described stages in human development and the ways in which the resolution of a development conflict at one stage will in turn affect the resolutions of subsequent development conflicts. The entire psychoanalytic theory from Freud to Horney to Sullivan is based on a series of developmental stages with the most crucial ones usually taking place before about age six. The resolution of each stage has consequences for subsequent stages. Similarly, other more eclectic descriptions of development (Havighurst, 1953; Gesell, 1945; Murray, 1938; Piaget, 1932) emphasize the early years as the base for later development.

Bloom's third reason why a child's early environment and early experiences are of crucial importance stems from the learning process. It is much easier to learn something new than it is to stamp out one set of learned behaviors and replace them with a new set. Although each learning theory may explain the phenomena in different ways, most theorists would agree that the initial learning a child receives takes place more easily than a later one that is contradicting some prior training or education. This is the same experience as learning a new language after adolescence and making characteristic mispronunciations the rest of your life. [3]

It is quite apparent that a child's first five or six years are the "foundation" years. It is imperative that a dependable guardian, preferably a parent, be the "builder" of this foundation. Spend time during these years being part of your child's world. These years are truly the cornerstone of his or her life and your relationship together. Try not to miss this unique opportunity.

While working at the YMCA, I happened to pick up a piece written by George Riggins.

> A mother was having a hard time getting her son to go to school one morning. "Nobody likes me at school," said the son. "The teachers don't and the kids don't. The superintendent wants to transfer me, the bus drivers hate me, the school board wants me to drop out, and the custodians have got it in for me. I don't want to go."
>
> "You've got to go," insisted the mother. "You're healthy, you have a lot to learn. You've got something to offer others. You are a leader. Besides, you are 49 years old and you're the principal.

This anecdote humorously attests to the fact that most adults do not feel good about themselves. A recent research report found that although 80 percent of children entering school have positive self-images, only 20 percent still do by the fifth grade, and only 5 percent feel good about themselves by the time they are high school seniors.[4] You need to be a major force in helping your child develop and maintain a positive self-image.

A positive self-image, high self esteem, a good self-concept, great self-worth—these words all mean believing in yourself. Having confidence is essential for a fulfilling life. How does a child gain confidence and feel good about herself or himself? Confidence and self-worth are gained when parents provide an atmosphere of love, joy, peace, patience, kindness, goodness, faithfulness, gentleness, and self-control. For self-esteem to blossom, a child must feel assurance from a parent or a care-giver that he or she is important.

While at a full-day seminar in New York City, my assistant and I decided to go out to lunch. Since it was a beautiful fall day, we took our sandwiches to a small corner park. As we walked down the streets, we noticed that people were looking at us, some smiling, others displaying perplexed expressions, still others nodding. Normally people will make little or no eye contact with passersby, but it wasn't until we sat down that I laughingly discovered why we were getting so much attention. We were still wearing our name tags from the seminar. Even in the busy streets of New York, small name tags caught the attention of those we passed and provoked a response.

Use this same imagery with your child. Imagine a sign on him or her which reads, "Please help me feel important!" Notice this sign every day and help fulfill this request in the form of praise, attention, understanding, challenges that can be met, guidance, encouragement, and love. These are the things that will help build your child's self-esteem.

START IS: SHAPING TOMORROW'S ADULTS BY REACHING OUT TODAY

DAY 3 : START understanding your role as a parent and its effect on your child, yourself, and those around you. This generates the needed appreciation, sensitivity, understanding, and insight in your new capacity.

Parenting Is Fulfilling

There was only going to be one performance. The parents knew this and allotted time in their busy schedules to attend. The show was a "once in a lifetime" performance. About 200 children, ages three to fifteen, would display their gymnastic talents in front of a crowd of over 1,000 family members and friends. On the big night, the atmosphere was charged with excitement. The participants were waiting anxiously to perform their gymnastic "circus acts."

Proud parents were easily identified by the glow of concentration as their children performed. Each parent was mesmerized as a "part of them" completed the gymnastic routine. The children were enthusiastic, the parents excited; the children apprehensive, the parents nervous; the children participating, the parents living.

After the show, the children displayed confidence and a feeling of accomplishment; the parents displayed satisfaction and a feeling of completeness. The children achieved success, while the parents achieved fulfillment.

This gymnastic show was organized by the Lakewood-Trumbull YMCA and presented at the Trumbull High School in Connecticut. It was the result of a year's work with children in all the levels of the gymnastics program. Sue Anderson, Program Director, had developed, choreographed and presented this show as the conclusion to the program year. Although the staff and children dedicated much to the performance, the parents also made their contributions. It was their commitment that made the event possible. Each parent chose to dedicate time to register their child for each session of classes, to motivate the child to attend class, to drive the child to class, to prepare for the show by making a costume, and to devote a Sunday afternoon for the performance. Was it worth it? For the child, it was pure joy to run to the parent after participating in the show. And if asked, each adult at the show would have responded emphatically, "I would not have missed this for anything in the world!" Parent involvement is evident in the many activities that children participate in, whether it be in a baseball game, a recital, a play, or a science fair. A parent's sense of fulfillment and pleasure is achieved by "being there."

Partake of the Community of Parents

Attending events such as the gymnastic show presents an opportunity for parents to be gathered with other parents. These circumstances are similar to a small "professional conference." Business and professional conventions provide:

• Inspiration and new ideas communicated by seminar speakers;

• Opportunities to gain and exchange ideas with other professionals in the field; and

• A chance to compare notes on problems and to be reassured that a solution is conceivable—that you are not the only one with that type of problem.

Raising children produces similar situations. You are involved with many parents in various situations such as extracurricular classes, visits to the doctor's office, school activities, sports events, or neighborhood activities. This network of parents provides inspiration and an arena for knowledge and comparisons. At times you may find yourself the "keynote speaker," helping another parent cope with or solve a difficult situation. In other circumstances you may need to be on the receiving end of some good advice. In any case, the parent community opens up an exciting new world. Make use of it and contribute to its rich exchange of ideas, communication, and opportunities.

S T A R T IS: SHAPING TOMORROW'S ADULTS BY REACHING OUT TODAY

DAY 4 : START engaging in life's adventures with your children. This is the first step to an enriching, lifelong relationship.

Enjoyment for You and Your Child

As a parent, you will have numerous opportunities to be a spectator in your child's life and view his or her participation in activities. But your child has a much more significant need and desire—a yearning to be with you. This is a yearning that can be satisfied when you participate in his or her activities, that is, when you play together.

Playing provides an opportunity to share time and grow with each other. It's a time for your child to enjoy new experiences and a time for you to introduce favorite activities from your own childhood. The opportunity for play takes place every day. Play experiences build a bond that becomes stronger with every encounter. You can experience the joy of being with your child in two significant ways: first by seeing the excitement and vigor in a child's eyes and smile, and second by sharing the best of your childhood by having fun yourself. Playing with a child is fun—enjoy it!

Lifetime Activities Start Today

We all know people who are in their thirties or forties who look and act as if they were well over a hundred, while there are many ninety-year-olds who have the energy, spirit, and drive of people in their twenties. People keep young by staying involved in activities and relationships. It also helps to have hope for the future. As children grow, their maturation provides endless opportunities for participation and companionship with adults. People need people, no matter what age. And people enjoy company with others that have similar interests. Developing and sharing common interests with your child makes growing older exciting and challenging. Lifetime activities such as tennis, golf, gardening, board games, crafts, and hobbies provide this link for lifelong parent-child relationships. It's important to your child, and it's vital to you.

Children—Our Future

"Growing up" has become a very disorienting, demanding, and pressure-filled course for today's youngsters. They are looking for stability, direction, and affection. When they don't find these, many children revert to drastic measures. An average of fourteen young people (below age twenty-four) kill themselves every day in the United States. Suicide is ranked as the second leading cause of death among young persons age fifteen to twenty-four.[5] As parents, we need to focus our energies and resources on providing a consistent, caring, and stimulating environment. It's a challenge we should wholeheartedly accept, dedicating an ample quantity of time to fulfill our children's needs.

Think about this. In 1993 there were over 70 million youngsters age nineteen and under in the United States. By the year 2010, it is estimated that this number may rise to over 83 million. Over 27 percent of the population will consist of youth, and they will eventually be responsible for 100 percent of our future. The elementary school age population (five to thirteen years of age) is projected to remain above the 1993 level for fifty years!

Linda Ching Sledge is a person who will affect the future of our youth in two ways. She is a "teacher" on two levels—a mother and a school instructor. She shares her insights on what it means to achieve "success."

> In mid-career, I suffered a failure of purpose. The joy and pain of teaching exhausted me. So on a trip back to Hawaii, my birthplace, I decided to capture the voices of my family on tape. I was looking for a way to measure the years, to test my idea of success and to feel less like a stranger to those I loved.
>
> Uncle Dennis was one of the first people I wanted to speak to. He had risen from office boy to president of Hawaii's largest bank corporation, and he possessed all the tokens of success—a beautiful home,

cars, and condominiums. It took me awhile to work up the nerve to call him, but he was glad to hear from me and immediately invited me to his office. After greeting me warmly, he urged me to begin.

Long after the tape ran out, we were still talking. He spoke not of his public successes but of his private tribulations. He described the shock of his young wife's fatal illness, the terror of being left a widower with small children, his love for his two daughters and two sons, and the hope that he had been a good enough parent over the years. Would he be the same if his wife had lived? He wondered. I sensed that he would have traded all he owned to have her by his side.

I gave him a hug and left, no longer feeling like a stranger.

Too often I expect vulnerability and doubt only from myself, not from others, especially those of prominence and wealth. What my uncle showed me is that time is not marked by years, but by joy and pain. And that success is not measured by what we own, but by how deeply we love.[6]

"One hundred years from now, it will not matter what kind of car I drove, what kind of house I lived in, how much I had in my bank account, nor what my clothes looked like. But the world may be a little better because I was important in the life of a child."

—*Author Unknown*

2

Developing a New and Improved Attitude

"I love having time for myself, but I love spending time with my child more."

—*Parent of a two-year-old child*

The statement above is very powerful and one that I can very easily affirm. But I didn't always feel this way. It took me longer than two years after our first child, Ryan, was born to reach this conclusion. During the first two years, I had a hard time giving up some of the things I liked to do by myself or with other people. I still wanted to get the foursome together for an evening of tennis. I wanted to improve my golf game. I needed to jog three times a week. I had a stack of magazines and books to read. There was so much work to be done around the house. Ryan would just have to work around my schedule—or so I thought.

After two years of parenting, I looked back on the overall experience. Things seemed to be getting easier. My wife, Sue, and I were now getting more sleep after tending to our colicky baby for his first nine months. Ryan could communicate better with us and also play alone for extended periods of time. We were able to take him with us more often. I was starting to find more time again—for me, that is. Parenting seemed to be working, but something was missing. I asked myself, "What do I want from this relationship with Ryan?" I realized full well what a child's needs really were and the important role I would have in preparing Ryan for adulthood, but what was I really looking for with him?

I wanted an enriching, lifelong relationship with my child. I wanted it to be exciting, zealous, animated, warm, and rewarding. And how would I obtain this, not only for now, but for the rest of my life? I realized, finally, that by devoting a relatively small amount of years right now, I would increase the closeness between us for a lifetime. I had to take advantage of opportunities that would allow my feelings and emotions to surface and be shared with Ryan. I knew that all of this was surely possible, and I knew that it was going to be entirely up to me.

Don't get me wrong—I still enjoy playing tennis and reading, and I certainly find time for myself. But now I'm enjoying time with my child, understanding why, and feeling good about it.

START IS: SHAPING TOMORROW'S ADULTS BY REACHING OUT TODAY

DAY 5 : START providing your child's needs with enthusiasm and a positive attitude. The enjoyable time you spend with your child improves your child's outlook on life as well as your view of your role as parent.

Parenting Is . . .

There are many changes that take place in your life when you become a parent. Comedian Bill Cosby, the father of five children, explains these changes in this way:

> My wife was a beautiful woman, before the children came. I've never met a more beautiful-looking woman—in the face, in the body, and in the mind—than my wife. Then the children came. And the curse began to take its toll. My wife's face began to change; the corners of her mouth dropped down, and when she talked, her eyebrows went up and down, and her right hand became deformed. And when she talked she would stick her finger out like this (pointing finger).[1]

This image of an adult physically and mentally changing gets a big laugh from the audience. Why? Because there is a great amount of truth to it. Raising children is tiring. Raising children is hard work. Raising children is frustrating. Raising children is a lifetime responsibility. This reality can be shocking and overwhelming, not only to the first-time parent, but also to experienced parents each time a child is born. Each child is different and demands a great deal from a parent for a successful upbringing.

Parenting Can Be . . .

Life always provides you with a choice. Parenting is no different. Raising children can be a very positive and enlightening experience. Or not. Parenting can be invigorating, pleasurable, and rewarding. Or not. It's your choice.

Is	*Can be*
•Tiring	•Invigorating
•Hard work	•Pleasurable
•Frustrating	•Rewarding
•Lifetime responsibility	•Lifetime relationship

You can make parenting more positive with enthusiasm, a positive attitude, an awareness of the value and innate worth of a child, and an endless amount of sharing—of feelings, hopes, dreams, and moments together. By changing your attitude, you will be giving yourself more opportunities and choices in your role as a parent. Again, it's your choice.

Enthusiasm

"A man can succeed at almost anything for which he has unlimited enthusiasm."

—Charles M. Schwab (1862-1939), American entrepreneur

Enthusiasm is electrifying. Enthusiasm is contagious. Enthusiasm is believing in what you are doing and exerting all your strength and feelings into the task. Enthusiasm produces results. Winning teams have it. Good sales people use it. Leaders display it. Entrepreneurs thrive on it. And it's in all of us.

To be enthusiastic, you have to act enthusiastically. When you wholeheartedly engage in an activity, your enthusiasm gives you new energy. Enthusiasm gives you the power to complete a job, to overcome an obstacle, or to have the most fulfilling experience possible. It's what you need to change the *tiring* obligation of parenting into an *invigorating* encounter with your children.

Positive Thinking

Positive thinking works. I've had the opportunity to work professionally with the "father" of positive thinking, the late Dr. Norman Vincent Peale. His bestseller, *The Power of Positive Thinking* has sold more than 15 million copies worldwide and has been translated into forty languages. At Guideposts Associates, Inc., one of my responsibilities is coordinating the recordings for Dial Guideposts for Inspiration. This telephone service provides callers with daily two-minute messages by Dr. and Mrs. Peale on a variety of topics. The messages focus on how to live a positive, faith-filled, and abundant life. This service provides inspiration to more than a million callers every year. And I receive numerous testimonials on how a positive attitude has made all the difference in overcoming a problem or situation. When I worked with Dr. Peale in a New York recording studio, you could not help but feel and absorb his positive attitude. The genuineness and intensity of his attitude was reflected and felt by all those involved with the recording, including the technicians.

Take this idea of positive thinking—thinking and believing you can achieve and then knowing and realizing you will—and apply it to growing with your children. Don't think of child raising as a tiring, exhausting, mundane activity. It can be an action-packed, fortifying experience. A positive attitude transforms *hard work* into a series of *pleasurable experiences*.

Beauty and Value

We've all heard the expression, "Beauty is in the eye of the beholder." This statement holds true for a subject like art. Each one of us has certain works of art that appeal to us. Today, art has not only become a thing of beauty, but also an investment. One of the most expensive pieces of art sold was Vincent Van Gogh's "Irises"—$ 53.9 million! As time goes on, this painting will surely increase in value.

Now consider a child. How does your child perceive her or his worth? Are there other "objects" in your life that seem to be more valuable than your child? Are you showing your child that she or he is worth more to you each day? Keep in mind that along with beauty, value "is in the eye of the beholder." Make every attempt to show your child that she or he is priceless! Convert the *frustrating* feelings that you inevitably will feel at times into a *rewarding* experience by recognizing daily the value and beauty of your child.

Lost Opportunities

Studies have shown that in order for children to lead productive lives, they must have the opportunity to establish a close bond with someone. This is good news! But who will this close person be? Who will experience the endless sharing of feelings, dreams, and special moments with your child? Make sure the opportunity to develop and strengthen your relationship with that special person—your child—is not lost. Be the one your child will reach out for and grow up with.

Harry Chapin in 1974 expressed this notion of a lost opportunity for a father and son in the following song, "Cats in the Cradle." The father in this song intends to spend time with his child but somehow actually doing so eludes him day by day, and then year by year. As these lyrics suggest, a parent must choose to take the *lifetime responsibility* of parenting and develop it into a *lifetime relationship*—today, before it's too late.

Cat's in the Cradle

by Harry Chapin (Copyright © 1974 by Story Songs, Ltd.)

My child arrived just the other day;
he came to the world in the usual way.
But there were planes to catch and bills to pay;
he learned to walk while I was away.
And he was talkin' 'fore I knew it,
and as he grew he'd say,
"I'm gonna be like you, Dad,
you know I'm gonna be like you."

And the cat's in the cradle and the silver spoon,
    little boy blue and the man in the moon.
"When you comin' home, Dad?"
"I don't know when, but we'll get together then;
you know we'll have a good time then."

My son turned ten just the other day;
he said, "Thanks for the ball, Dad, come on let's play.
Can you teach me to throw?"
I said, "Not today, I got a lot to do."
He said, "That's okay."
And he walked away, but his smile never dimmed,
it said, "I'm gonna be like him, yeah,
you know I'm gonna be like him."

And the cat's in the cradle and the silver spoon,
    little boy blue and the man in the moon.
"When you comin' home, Dad?"
"I don't know when, but we'll get together then;
you know we'll have a good time then."

Well, he came from college just the other day;
so much like a man I just had to say,
"Son, I'm proud of you, can you sit for awhile?"
He shook his head and he said with a smile,
"What I'd really like, Dad, is to borrow the car keys;
see you later, can I have them please?"

And the cat's in the cradle and the silver spoon,
     little boy blue and the man in the moon.
"When you comin' home, Dad?"
"I don't know when, but we'll get together then;
you know we'll have a good time then."

I've long since retired, my son's moved away;
I called him up just the other day. I said,
"I'd like to see you if you don't mind."
He said, "I'd love to, Dad, if I can find the time.
You see, my new job's a hassle, and the kids have the flu,
but it's sure nice talkin' to you."
And as I hung up the phone, it occurred to me,
he'd grown up just like me;
my boy was just like me.

And the cat's in the cradle and the silver spoon,
     little boy blue and the man in the moon.
"When you comin' home, Dad?"
"I don't know when, but we'll get together then;
you know we'll have a good time then."

START IS: SHAPING TOMORROW'S ADULTS BY REACHING OUT TODAY

DAY 6 : START "giving up" some of your personal time for your family. "Sacrifices" produce winning teams (families) and a better functioning society.

The all-American sport of baseball has some interesting plays and strategies. As a child, I could never quite understand a "sacrifice bunt." I surely did not want to be the one who would be put out. But I later learned the rationale behind this play. The batter who hit the "sacrifice bunt" was doing something for the good of the team. His effort improved the scoring possibility of the runner already on base. It is a winning strategy that means helping someone else by giving up something of yourself. As a parent, what you may be giving up is personal time, convenience, and energy; you may even dramatically change your lifestyle to help your child.

In our family, 1955 was a very significant year. My parents and their three children were attempting to leave the Russian-occupied city of Leipzig, East Germany. Many families had made the decision to leave because the future they were offered there was unacceptable. The government was quickly stifling the opportunities for additional families to leave. My mother made a reconnaissance trip to West Berlin. Upon returning, she and my father made the life-changing decision to attempt to leave Leipzig, a sacrifice that was not understood then by their three small children. My parents were leaving a successful business, their careers, family and friends, and the place that they called home. The subsequent trip to West Berlin was successful, but my parents had left with only the clothes on their back. After finding temporary refuge in Altenstadt, a small town in the mountains of southern Germany, they made the decision to go to the United States. They arrived with very little money, three children (and another child on the way), a language difficulty, no contacts, and no jobs. Still, my parents were excited about starting a new life.

Mom and Dad sacrificed a familiar lifestyle in return for the opportunity to provide a proper family environment for us all to grow together. Each person makes sacrifices at different points in life. Whenever a family is involved, every decision made by a parent will have an effect on all family members. Only you will be able to evaluate your family's life situation and decide on any sacrifice that may be necessary. This is not always an easy task, but one that you as a parent will frequently be faced with.

Millions of people have had the pleasure of seeing Radio City Music Hall's Christmas Show in New York City. It's a live two-hour display of the joys of Christmas. The final act is a moving reenactment of the birth of Jesus, with an extravagant procession of people, animals, and props.

A similar reenactment takes place each year in St. Joseph's Church in upstate New York, which our family attends on Christmas Eve. The props are simple—a wooden crib, bags of straw, and a baby doll. Interested children of all ages fill the wooden cradle with straw and create a circle around it. The baby is placed in the crib to signify the birth of Jesus. The Nativity story is read. This spectacle is performed each year and is a very special part of our family's Christmas celebration, not only for the children, but Sue and me, too. When our son, Ryan, first walked up and placed his handful of straw in the cradle and took a place in the circle, it evoked an indescribable feeling of joy and gratification. The intensity of these feelings cannot be created by any producer; they must be experienced personally. This sort of bearing witness to a child's development takes place throughout a child's maturation years, but you as a parent must grasp these opportunities and become actively involved in them.

Quality Time

"Quality time. Your moments together are too precious to waste." A recent ad for audio equipment shows a father simultaneously holding a baby and listening through headphones to a compact disc. I realize the ad is selling electronic equipment, but the picture is not so out of line in today's "me first" society.

A study surveying 1,500 households was conducted by the noted Institute for Social Research at the University of Michigan. The findings reveal that:

- Mothers working outside the home spend an average of eleven minutes a day on weekdays, and thirty minutes a day on weekends with the children. (These figures do not include mealtime.)

• Homemaker mothers spend an average of thirty minutes a day on weekdays and thirty-six minutes a day on weekends with the children. (This may reflect the fact that children of homemaker mothers were younger and needed more attention.)

• Fathers spend an average of eight minutes a day on weekdays and fourteen minutes a day on weekends in different activities with their children. (It did not make a difference whether their wives worked or not.) [2]

In March 1986, the U.S. Department of Education released *What Works: Research About Teaching and Learning*. This booklet contained forty-one findings from some of the best research about what works when it comes to educating a child. The second edition, released in 1987, contains an additional eighteen findings. The information in this booklet is a distillation of a large body of scholarly research in the field of education. *What Works* concluded that "American mothers on average spend less than half an hour a day talking, explaining, or reading with their children. Fathers spend less than fifteen minutes." [3]

Can this amount of time, even if it is entirely "focused" or "concentrated" on a child, be adequate for the child?

Quality time has become an overused, unclear term to describe the precious moments parents share with their children. I have a hard time using this phrase because it implies a number of negative connotations.

Quality time implies that you are making time for your child in a manner that makes it seem like an obligation rather than a priority. Spending time with your children is a privilege and a delight, not something you should "fit into your schedule if you can." It is not the "leftover time." Some parents feel a small amount of time adequately fulfills a child's needs. "One-minute parenting" may be convenient for the parent, but it simply does not meet the requirements of a child.

Quality time implies that a set amount of time will produce the best times, the needed experiences, and the essential parental feelings. In reality, "memorable times" happen unexpectedly, and the frequency with which they occur is proportionate to the amount of time spent with a child. The more time you spend with your child, the more significant the experiences and the more intense your relationship.

The Parent/Child Formula

A quantity of time with your child
+
A high intensity of positive interaction
=
Memorable experiences
=
Gratification and growth
=
Better relationship and bond with child
=
Well-adjusted child
=
Well-adjusted adult
=
Better functioning society

The *quantity* of time you spend as a parent participating in activities that foster a positive relationship with your child contributes in significant ways to the shaping of a productive and well-adjusted adult. Take the *quantity time* necessary to make a strong bond between you and your child. It will be gratifying for both of you, and that will ultimately benefit society as a whole.

S T A R T IS: SHAPING TOMORROW'S ADULTS BY REACHING OUT TODAY

DAY 7 : START realizing that if you give your child your undivided attention, **you** will both enjoy the time together. Spending time together will give you and your child many satisfying and gratifying experiences.

A Child's Available Time

"If only I had done it differently" is the common lament of many letters written to Ann Landers and other columnists. In the following testimony, a father looks back and realizes the special opportunity he has lost as a parent.

Dear Ann Landers: A number of my friends work so many hours that they rarely see their children. When they finally make the time, they discover that their children are grown up and have no time for them.

I wrote the following piece and you are welcome to share it with your readers if you think it's good enough.

Where Did the Years Go?

I remember talking to my friend a number of years ago about our children. Mine were five and seven then, just the ages when their daddy means everything to them. I wished that I could have spent more time with my kids but I was too busy working. After all, I wanted to give them all the things I never had when I was growing up.

I loved the idea of coming home and having them sit on my lap and tell me about their day. Unfortunately, most days I came home so late that I was only able to kiss them good night after they had gone to sleep.

It is amazing how fast kids grow. Before I knew it, they were nine and eleven. I missed seeing them in school plays. Everyone said they were terrific, but the plays always seemed to go on when I was traveling for business or tied up in a special conference. The kids never complained, but I could see the disappointment in their eyes.

I kept promising that I would have more time "next year." But the higher up the corporate ladder I climbed, the less time there seemed to be.

Suddenly they were no longer nine and eleven. They were fourteen and sixteen. Teenagers. I didn't see my daughter the night she went out on her first date or my son's championship basketball game. Mom made excuses and I managed to telephone and talk to them before they left the house. I could hear the disappointment in their voices, but I explained as best I could.

Don't ask where the years have gone. Those little kids are nineteen and twenty-one now and in college. I can't believe it. My job is less demanding and I finally have time for them. But they have their own interests and there is no time for me. To be perfectly honest, I'm a little hurt.

It seems like yesterday that they were five and seven. I'd give anything to live those years over. You can bet your life I'd do it differently. But they are gone now, and so is my chance to be a real dad.

Sign me—Lonely, Anywhere, U.S.A.

Dear Lonely: It's excellent. You've zeroed in on one of the principal problems of parenthood in the '80s (and '90s). Thanks for tossing it my way.[4]

Let's look at the reality of how a child's time is used and how a child's "available time" for parents greatly diminishes as he or she grows older.

Your Child's Available Time

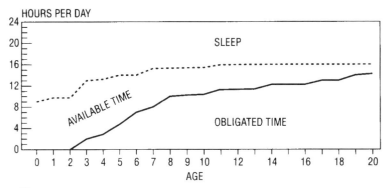

Key:
- *Sleep—resting hours of child, including naps*
- *Obligated Time—time your children will be spending at school, sports, lessons and instructional classes, with friends, and a job*
- *Available Time—amount of time your child has left*

From birth to age four, children sleep eleven to fifteen hours a day. But when they are not sleeping, they are completely available to you, other than the time they are in nursery school. You may not be available, but your child is and would like to be with anyone who will give him or her the time.

Children aged five to ten generally require eight to ten hours of sleep. When a child reaches the age of five or six, school begins to consume four to eight hours a day. As a child matures, reaching seven to ten years, he or she becomes more preoccupied with school and starts becoming involved in after-school sports and other extracurricular activities. Peers become more important and children start to spend more time with their friends.

Extracurricular activities and friendships continue to play a major role for children from ages eleven to sixteen, although they do need less sleep (eight hours) by this age.

Once teenagers get a driver's license at the age of sixteen, driving and dating begin to enter into the teen's life. And if your "child" is still home by age eighteen to twenty, the time he or she may have available for you will most likely be no more than some one or two hours a day—if you're lucky.

Unfortunately, some parents may think, "I will spend more time with children when they grow up." Just the opposite is true. You make more time for *them*, but unfortunately they start to have less time for *you*. When is the right time to be with them? NOW! Start when your child is born. The first six years is when your child has the most available time for you. And as your child continues to grow, make it a priority to play an active role in his or her available time—whatever amount of time is available. It's never too late to start.

Special Attention

The opportunities are always there for you to get actively involved with your child. Whatever your child's age, time is available if you think about it and take advantage of those special moments. Here are a few examples:

From Infancy through Age Two

- More than 6,000 *diaper-changing opportunities*
- More than 3,000 *bottle and feeding opportunities*
- More than 2,000 *daily walk or child-care transportation times*

For Toddlers, Ages Three to Six

- Available for interaction with parents *seven to twelve hours* a day, this age group allows an *unlimited amount of activities*.
- More than 1,000 *meals per year* to be shared
- 365 *mornings* to start together
- 365 *bedtimes* for reading to the child or time to recount the day's events together
- 52 *full weekends* per year
- Monthly *holidays* to be celebrated
- If your child goes to school or day care, 400-500 *drop-off and pick-up days*

During Adolescence, Ages Seven to Twelve

- *Preparing meals* together

- *Doing chores* together

- *Participating in or viewing sports events*

- *Watching movies together*

- *Becoming involved with school work* as a sounding board or by offering support

- *Taking trips* that will be cherished for a lifetime

Grandparents

If you are fortunate enough to have active, loving grandparents nearby, they may want to become involved in some of the above activities. Grandparents can be such special people in the lives of children. Their title alone signifies their important role—*grand*. Grandparents who value their new role and play an active part in their grandchild's upbringing develop a close relationship with that child. An involved grandparent realizes the innate importance of each grandchild, is genuinely interested in the child, and is willing to share her or his love abundantly. Also, grandparents are usually in a position where more "free time" is available. Grandparents can take advantage of this luxury and make spending time with their grandchild a priority. This combination of undivided attention, emotional intimacy, and shared time produces a strong affectionate bond. Just keep in mind that a relationship with a grandparent can never be a substitute for your child's relationship with *you*.

Going the Extra Mile

Certain American Indian tribes believe strongly that all life's activities and experiences are circular—day follows night and winter becomes spring. What you give out, you get back at some later time; it all comes around full circle. As the Bible says, what you sow, you shall reap. Think of all that you do as an echo. What you send out comes back to you. Put these beliefs and truths to work in your relationship with your child. Go that extra mile.

Invest $5-$10 on an appointment book, if you do not have one already. Among the meetings, doctor's appointments, and car repairs, schedule in time for your children. Make it a daily commitment for the next fourteen days, *in addition to the normal time you spend with your children*. Here are some guidelines:

- Set aside a realistic amount of time that you will be able to dedicate to your children and adhere to it—no excuses.

- Use this time to help you identify your children as a priority, and get into a routine of spending more time with them.

- While spending time with your children, think about the degree to which you really are involved with them. (For help in evaluating this, see the next section.)

START IS: SHAPING TOMORROW'S ADULTS BY REACHING OUT TODAY

DAY 8 : START striving for active participation and open communication with your child. You will develop a close personal tie with your child as a result.

What Level Are You On?

I hope my kids take me to Disney World again soon! Our last family vacation to the Magic Kingdom gave us all a tremendous number of memories. For me, the most vivid experiences were family activities. These included enjoying a Disney breakfast together on the Empress Lilly and meeting all the Disney characters, running around the playground area in Mickey Mouse's Birthdayland, buying and playing with a six-piece Matchbox construction truck set (Ryan's major souvenir selection), and digging in a sandbox at Sea World. You may wonder why these particular experiences stand out so strongly from all the other attractions. We enjoyed all the shows, rides and displays, but the family interaction that took place was most memorable.

Spending time with your child means becoming *involved* with them, and there are numerous ways to be involved. One major aspect of involvement is the level of communication you have with your child—very little, a modest amount, a considerable amount, or an abundant amount. Communication, the skill of talking *and* listening, is the cornerstone of a strong bond with your child. Another involvement connection is how closely you and your child participate in an activity. Participating together means working or playing on a similar project or activity, becoming partners, striving for an analogous goal. Participation may be more individual; you may interact as colleagues (swimming at a beach) or spectators (viewing a movie together).

Let's look more closely at what I call the Four Levels of Involvement with your child:

I. BEING THERE is the first step to being with your child. Just being present and available (if needed) provides assurance to your child. At this level, communication may be limited to little or no conversation. Examples: watching a sleeping baby, working on a project while your child works on another, reading while your child plays nearby.

II. SIDE BY SIDE is when you and your child work together in close proximity. Communication broadens to exchanging thoughts, feelings, and ideas at various intervals. Each of you may check on the other's progress. Examples: doing related chores such as washing the car while your child washes a bike, watching TV together, reading side by side.

III. COMPANIONSHIP is when you and your child play, build, create, or just enjoy the same activity together. At this involvement level, which is usually of short duration (less than one hour), there is considerable sharing of thoughts, feelings, and actions. Examples: coloring or reading together, playing with toys together, planting a garden together.

IV. UNITED refers to a parent-child experience that allows your relationship to really flourish. Becoming "united" with your child takes place over the course of more time than is required at the other levels. There is an abundant sharing of experiences, interests, and desires. Examples: trips, camp outs, parent-child tournaments, cooking, time-intensive chores such as rearranging a room.

I remembered our trip to Disney World so well because my child and I could interact at the Companionship and United levels. It is important to be aware of your level of involvement and the level you are striving for during activities with your child. There are appropriate times for each of these levels of interaction. It would be too intense to participate at the Companionship and United levels all the time. But remember that those are the levels that yield emotionally uplifting results and memorable experiences.

Too Much Time?

A group of researchers and clinicians known as *attachment theorists* have studied the infant-mother (child-parent) bond for more than twenty years. Although their scientific findings have been met with some opposition, Mary Slater Ainsworth and John Bowlby have provided strong evidence that a child's emotional stability is linked to her or his need for an early attachment or bond with a parent. Researchers, government agencies, and parents question exactly how much time is needed to best serve a child's emotional needs. While there is no precise answer, there is no question that for a relationship to flourish, a parent should spend an abundant amount of positive interaction time with a child.

Some parents wonder if they are spending too much time with their child. Take this quick six-question test to explore that possibility:

1. Am I working outside the home, either for pay or as a volunteer?
2. Am I attending school or furthering my education?
3. Am I enjoying some activities without my child?
4. Am I spending time with friends and relatives without my child?
5. Does my child spend time alone with other children?
6. Does my child have alone time for him- or herself?

If you answered "no" to all six questions, it is a possibility that you may need more time for yourself. Otherwise, continue to enjoy the time you're spending with your child.

Several years ago I was working toward my Masters of Science degree in Computer Science. One evening during class I feared I wouldn't get to see my son off to bed that evening. I had expected to get out of class at 9:15, which meant I wouldn't be home until 10:00 p.m.—Ryan would be long asleep. But the class was let out early and I drove to my in-laws, where my wife and son were visiting. When I reached their house, everyone had gone out shopping and then to the playground.

I decided to give my mother a call while I waited. She answered the phone, and right away I knew something was wrong. She sounded like she had been crying. I asked her what was wrong, and she admitted that she was feeling desperately lonely. Although our family kept in continuous communication by phone, letters, and visits whenever possible, it was the first week my mother had been physically alone in over forty years. In the past eighteen months she had suffered many losses. My father had passed away; my mother had to sell the house she had lived in for twenty-five years; my oldest brother, his wife, and their two children had left for a two-year stay in Germany; and my younger brother, Peter, had just started school at Old Dominion University in Virginia. My mother was going to be by herself.

After comforting Mom, I hung up thinking about how she was feeling alone after raising five children. How quickly time passes! Then I was brought back to life by a familiar voice: "Dad, how was class?" I responded with a big hug, then after a quick bath for Ryan, we headed home. Ryan had decided to ride with me, with Sue following us in her car. Ryan and I started to talk during our ride, but I knew he was going to fall asleep soon. After checking to see if Sue was still following us, Ryan nodded off, clutching my finger in his hand. Truly, this was a sensational time to be sharing with my son.

It's your choice—you can make the time to be with your child. Take advantage of the opportunities to be together whenever they present themselves.

"Time flies, but remember, you're the navigator."

—*St. Louis Bugle*

CHAPTER

3

Tomorrow I'll Make Some
Time for My Child

"In making a living today, many no longer have room for life."

— *Joseph R. Sizzo*

I was driving to work one Monday morning thinking about the upcoming Labor Day weekend. It was going to be one of those "time for me" weekends. I was heading up to the Adirondacks with a friend for three days of hiking. Sue would be visiting her sister and taking Ryan to visit his cousin, Danny, in Albany. Sue had expressed concern about my safety while hiking in the Adirondacks—which I appreciated—but I was much more concerned about Ryan's safety. The house he would stay at was on a river and near a busy road. Unfortunately there was no protective fence. I had a chilling thought of something terrible happening to Ryan. . . . I flashed out of that solemn thought to the line of traffic ahead on Interstate 84. After a few frustrating minutes crawling along the road, I became aware of what had happened—a three-car accident. It must have just occurred because there was no police or ambulance. As I drove by, I thought, "What if something really happened to Ryan? Or to me? Did I spend enough time with my child? How would he remember me? What did we do last together? Had we exchanged our usual hugs and kisses on this busy Monday?

I realized with relief that even though it had been a hectic morning, I had found time for Ryan. We had done a few special things together.

Ryan decided we should make orange juice. This is usually part of our weekend ritual, but I had said, "Why not do it today?" My attitude was that this was important, extremely important, to do today. So we did it. It probably took three or four minutes, but they were truly special minutes for both of us. And of course before leaving, it was time for H's and K's, hugs and kisses. And the last words I heard Ryan yelling out the window were, "Be careful, Dad."

The possibility of either you or your child becoming critically injured or worse is highly unlikely, but think about it. What's important to you now? Does your child know you, and do you know your child? Did you give him or her child some attention this morning? When was the last time you both did something special together? Yesterday? Last week? Could it have been last month? Ask yourself, *Did I find enough time for my child?* Telling yourself, I'll find time for my child tomorrow, will not suffice in life-and-death situations.

Hopefully, you now find the time for your loved ones. If you don't, take a look at your schedule and your child's schedule. What are your priorities right now? Are they what you want them to be? What's important to you?

S T A R T IS: SHAPING TOMORROW'S ADULTS BY REACHING OUT TODAY

DAY 9 : START designating time with your child and your family as a high priority. Making this investment today will bring tomorrow's dividends.

What's My Schedule Look Like?

We've all heard people say, "I wish I could find the time for that," or, "There's never enough time in the day." Each person is working with the same number of minutes a day—1,440 minutes to be precise. We all know people who seem to do so much more than we do each day. What are you doing? It's important to look at your schedule and see how you are spending your time. Take a few of today's 1,440 minutes and complete the chart on page 50 to find out how you spend the seven days of a typical week.

After completing your regular schedule, complete an "ideal week." How would you really like to spend your time? Employment must be included in your ideal week if it is an economic necessity for you and the family. But there are ways to lessen your time at work, if you want to. In addition, economic necessity must be evaluated as "real" or "perceived." You need to realistically evaluate the essential priorities in your life. Be sure to include your child!

Bridging the Gap

We all have our idea of what would be an "ideal" schedule, one that would include spending more time with our family, but how do we reach it? Striving to reach the ideal week is dependent on believing wholeheartedly that "my family is important enough for me to give them the best of me *now*," and "I want to make more of my time available to them." *Making the time* is much different than *finding the time*. You will never quite find the time, because there's always something that will fill your schedule if you let it.

USA Today interviewed time experts to find out how many hours in a typical weekday would be needed to meet the amount of hours required for optimally completing twenty daily activities. When the recommended schedules and times were tabulated, the results showed that a person would need almost *forty-two* hours each day. Guess what? We obviously cannot meet these expectations. The solution to your time dilemma lies in adapting your attitude and making the time for your family by using any available time most effectively.

As I go to work, I cross a two-mile-long bridge over the Hudson River. The original bridge had four lanes—two westbound and two eastbound. As the population grew, traffic quickly became a problem and people were having a difficult time reaching their goal—the other side. A second span was built. This allowed the four lanes of the original span to be used solely for eastbound traffic, significantly improving the flow of cars. The continued success of this situation is the ongoing use of all four lanes. In bridging the gap from your typical week to your ideal week, you can take four routes or approaches, which will become a road that takes you closer to your ideal week:

1. Establish your priorities
2. Set some goals
3. Maximize your use of time
4. Minimize time-wasters

1. Establish Your Priorities

Everyone makes the time (and usually finds the money) for the activities they really want to do. Whether consciously or unconsciously, we all establish priorities in our lives. Each day we choose how we spend time—by ourselves, for other people, or with family and friends.

In looking back at your day yesterday, what were your priorities? Perhaps this list covers some of the items from your day:

- Doing activities with your family
- Entertainment (movies, theater, concerts, etc.)
- Exercising
- Helping others
- Meals
- Participating in religious activities
- Personal time (grooming, dressing, commuting, alone time)
- Reading
- Shopping
- Social activities (lunches, dinners, parties)
- Sports
- Traveling
- Visiting friends
- Watching television
- Working

You are the best judge of which activities are true necessities. You are in control. You have the power of choice. You make the decision about how much your children are included in your life and what activities you share together.

Use the following charts to first log your actual weekly activities ("Your Typical Week"), then prioritized your life and set realistic goals for how you will use your time ("Your Ideal Week").

YOUR TYPICAL WEEK (ACTUAL EXPERIENCE)

Activity	MON	TUE	WED	THU	FRI	SAT	SUN	TOTAL HOURS
Meals								
Sleep								
Personal Care								
Employment								
Chores/Errands								
Travel/Commuting								
Exercise								
Education								
Time with Family								
Leisure Activities								
Religious/Volunteer Activities								
	24	24	24	24	24	24	24	168

Round to the nearest quarter hour (increments of 15 minutes—.25 hour). Your total for each day must equal 24 hours; your weekly total must equal 168 hours.

YOUR IDEAL WEEK (GOALS/PRIORITIES)

Activity	MON	TUE	WED	THU	FRI	SAT	SUN	TOTAL HOURS
Meals								
Sleep								
Personal Care								
Employment								
Chores/Errands								
Travel/Commuting								
Exercise								
Education								
Time with Family								
Leisure Activities								
Religious/Volunteer Activities								
	24	24	24	24	24	24	24	168

Round to the nearest quarter hour (increments of 15 minutes—.25 hour). Your total for each day must equal 24 hours; your weekly total must equal 168 hours.

DAY 10 : START "making today count" and develop a lasting and fulfilling relationship with your family. Enjoy today together
and you will create a well-established family with a sound
future.

At work I've observed two fathers who talk a lot about the importance of family in their lives. The feelings they express, however, only
reveal part of the story, because their priorities are easily visible in the
way they choose to spend their time.

One man—I'll call him John—has three children. John expresses
the importance of spending time with his children, but he also demonstrates it. He works ten hours a day, five days a week—six, whenever
needed. John attends all the games and shows that his children participate in, and he usually volunteers to help coach the sports teams.
Many times this involves changing his work schedule. Summer vacation means spending a week or two on Cape Cod with his family.

John's colleague—let's call him Bill—has two children. Bill verbally expresses great interest in his children, but he always seems to
say, "I've got so much to do. I'll spend time with them this weekend.
They'll understand." Bill works twelve to fourteen hours a day, usually six days a week—by choice. One evening, Bill informed me he had
to make sure he got home early because it was his son's birthday. As
the evening went on, Bill became involved in many calls and meetings that could have waited until the next day. Finally at 9:00 P.M.,
Bill rushed out saying, "I didn't even have time to get him a present. I'll
spend time this weekend with him." When Bill and his wife spent
their last vacation in the Caribbean, it was explained as a "business
meeting." The children stayed with their grandparents. Bill explained,
"The weekend we get back, we are going on a family trip." But the
next weekend came and went without a trip with his children.

Whenever I think of Bill, I again think of Harry Chapin's song,
"Cat's in the Cradle," and I feel sorry for him and his family. Clearly Bill
has lost valuable time with his children, but I'm hoping he will soon
realize that he is missing the chance for a vibrant parenting experience. Bill needs to rearrange his priorities and integrate all parts of his

life. Hopefully, this will take place without the impetus of a life-threatening situation like the one that affected Orville Kelly.

Make Today Count

In the spring of 1974, Orville Kelly discovered he had lymphoma, a form of cancer. He was notified that he might have as little as six months, or as long as three years, to live.

After several months of chemotherapy, Orville realized that the depression and tension cancer had brought into his life were destroying his remaining days. More importantly, they were ruining his relationship with his family.

Orville decided that a new attitude of "grab each day as it comes, make the most of it, explore it to the fullest, enjoy all its delights and treasures" was needed. Orville felt so strong about this new attitude that he started a club for people facing a life-threatening illness. The first meeting was held on January 25, 1974, in the Burlington (Iowa) Elks Lodge. The eighteen people who attended decided to call their group Make Today Count (MTC). There are now over 300 chapters of MTC nationwide.

Orville realized that this new attitude helped his family—his wife, Wanda; Mark, thirteen; Tammy, eleven; Lori, eight; Britt, four; and himself—cope with his cancer and enjoy the remaining time they would be sharing.

Adopt this positive attitude when you plan your life with your family. Realize that for your child, today is the most important day. Plan for it. Enjoy it. Make it count.

S T A R T IS: SHAPING TOMORROW'S ADULTS BY REACHING OUT TODAY

DAY 11 : START setting short- and long-term goals. This will allow you to make the kinds of adjustments and commitments you need to make to spend more time with your child.

2. Set Some Goals

After analyzing your priorities, you'll be ready to take the second step. Setting some goals is an essential part of organizing and enjoying your life, whether at work or at home. Have you ever bowled, shot darts, or played golf? Imagine if someone took "goals" away from those activities. There would be no pins to aim at or knock over, no numbered areas to shoot at, or holes to keep you interested. It's the "goal" of bowling a strike, throwing a bull's-eye or shooting par that makes those activities challenging, intriguing, and fun.

Goals provide the map for your journey through life. All goal-setting entails four basic steps:

1. *Be specific.* Include a timetable for anticipated completion. Describe what you want to do in detail, using a newspaper reporter's Who, What, Where, Why, When, and How. Include short-term goals, which include anything in the coming year, and long-range goals, your hopes for the next two or ten years.

2. *Put it in writing.* Write down the information from Step 1, indicating the action steps needed to achieve your goal.

3. *Do it.* After your plans have been finalized, the next step is to carry them out!

4. *Evaluate, adapt, and revise (EAR).* Your goals will constantly change due to various circumstances and situations. It is important to evaluate your goals and, if need be, to adapt or revise them.

Use this goal-setting process to concentrate on the future growth of your family. Make sure you also consult with your partner or spouse to jointly go over your goals. It is important to mesh your goals when setting a course for a family, particularly for two-parent, two-job couples. The decisions you make will set an example for your child. Your attitude and your goals will tell your child what you think of family and social relationships, what your values and your spiritual beliefs are, how important your career and your financial status are relative to him or her, and how important it is to be physically fit. What is the message you want to convey to your child?

Goal-Setting in Action

After one of our weekly racquetball games, my partner Mike and I became involved in a discussion about the outdoors. We talked about our hiking experiences and learned that even though we lived so close to the Catskill Mountains, neither of us had done much hiking in that area. Being avid hikers, we planned a day hike in the region. We chose three peaks for our excursion, including the highest peak in the Catskills, Slide Mountain.

During the twelve hours on the trails, we came across information in one of the trail books about a hiking club in the area called the 3500 Club. After a very absorbing day of hiking, we decided to find out more about this club. We learned that their objective was to stimulate hiking in the Catskill region, and that the goal of club members was to climb thirty-eight peaks. These included thirty-four peaks higher than 3,500 feet plus four of these same peaks needed to be climbed again during the winter months. It sounded exciting, but doing all that seemed too big a task to me.

Because Mike and I had enjoyed our first Catskill excursion so much, we scheduled another hike a month or so later. After the second hike, we realized we had already completed six peaks. We decided the task of completing the thirty-eight peaks within the time limit for the 3500 Club would be achievable. Mike and I carefully mapped out future hikes with anticipated dates. We later made some date changes and revised hiking agendas, yet we made every effort to stick to our overall plan. Two years later, Mike and I completed the thirty-eight peaks, walking more than 175 miles in sixteen hikes. This included one hike in snow drifts more than five-feet deep, with a wind chill factor of forty degrees below zero. Officially, I became the 588th person on record to achieve the 3,500 hiking feat.

Mike and I are currently involved in a new adventure. As members of the 46er's Club, we have climbed fifteen of the forty-six peaks higher than 4,000 feet in the Adirondacks. In the future, I plan to hike the Catskill peaks again, this time with my family. Looking at long-range plans, there is a new club called the High Pointers, which sets an objective of climbing the highest points in all fifty states. As of this writing, only eleven people have completed this undertaking!

Goals are synonymous with achievement. Dream, plan, and accomplish your goals.

Going the Extra Mile

After completing Your Typical Week and Your Ideal Week charts, ask someone in your life—a partner, relative, friend, or co-worker to look at your goals and help you revamp your schedule to meet them. Above all else, be receptive to their positive feedback.

Guidelines:

•Consider all options for helping you meet your time and achievement goals. Write them down.

•Do not become judgmental of any ideas your "helper" suggests.

•Put two or three of these ideas into action—those to which you know you can make a commitment.

§ T A R T IS: SHAPING TOMORROW'S ADULTS BY REACHING OUT TODAY

DAY 12 : START reorganizing your daily schedule by utilizing "time-savers" and controlling "time-wasters" to accommodate the time you want to spend with your family. This will alleviate much stress, frustration, confusion, and guilt in the future.

3. Maximize Your Use of Time

Work seems to be the number one stumbling block for spending time with children. A recent study of two-parent, two-job families showed that 73 percent would have one parent stay at home if money were not a factor (which meant they were working out of economic necessity or perceived economic necessity). If this is the case, let's take a look at the possibilities if a parent desires to remain at home:

•*Working at home.* Can your work be completed in a home setting, at least on a temporary basis?

- *Taking a leave of absence or sabbatical.* Will your company allow this type of time off?

- *Part-time work.* This is a viable alternative for a wide variety of positions.

- *Telecommuting.* Can the telephone, fax machine, and personal computer be set up in your home with a linkup to the main office systems?

If these changes are not feasible, let's look at other options. The following alternative work times are now options for more than a fifth of the American work force, according to a report by the Work in America Institute:

- *Flextime*—flexible starting and quitting times

- *Compressed work schedule or block scheduling*—working a full forty-hour "week" in less than five days

- *Job sharing*—having two part-time people sharing the responsibilities of one full-time person

- *V-time*—a voluntary, temporary reduction in working hours

Invest time now in finding out what options are available at your workplace. Pursue the avenues that would best meet both your needs and your employer's.

Twenty Time-Saving Techniques

Perhaps none of the above work options is possible for you. If that's the case, try to make best use of your work schedule to give you extra time at home with your child.

The following management techniques will give you opportunities to improve your work performance and reduce your work time. Several of these suggestions may be obvious, but sometimes working on the basics is the key to improved time management. Use the techniques that will work for you.

- Keep one appointment book for all work, family, and social appointments for easy and accurate appointment scheduling. When family activities are noted with work-related appointments, they are less likely to be lost or forgotten.

- Use a "To Do" list on a weekly and daily basis for work and home tasks; include priorities and time estimates for maximum time allocations and usage. Remember that your child has a "To Do" List, too—things to do *with you*. Keep your child on your daily list!

- Find out when your peak working time is—morning or afternoon—and complete your most important and difficult tasks then.

- Keep your workplace neat and organized for instant retrieval of information.

- Establish blocks of time for "no calls, no visits" for uninterrupted concentration on work projects.

- Examine and analyze the work flow through your office, and look for ways to simplify it.

- Maintain a proper working atmosphere—a functional desk, comfortable chair, easy-to-reach phone, and comfortable room temperature for most effective work habits. A family photo is a definite requirement for your desk.

- If possible, delegate work to properly trained and appropriate co-workers to free up your time for meeting necessary additional responsibilities on a timely basis.

- Have your calls screened to lessen unnecessary interruptions.

- Recognize, analyze, manage, or conquer procrastination by setting a goal to save an extra five to ten minutes a day.

- Make use of bulletin boards for easy viewing of schedules and updates on present projects.

- Learn from co-workers, managers, and executives how they successfully manage their time. Be sure to seek out those who clearly have established their family as a priority.

- Make use of commuting time for brainstorming, planning, and organizing work ideas and upcoming family activities.

- Know and use the capabilities of your phone, the company's fax machine, and other business machines, too, like computers, photocopiers, dictation machines, calculators, etc.—especially the computer and specialized software programs!

Here are five techniques to help you deal with the tremendous amount of paperwork we all have.

- •Touch papers once. As you handle each document, use one of the following DRAFT actions: Delegate, Read, Act, File, or Toss.

- •Keep active files handy. Use the 80/20 rule. Eighty percent of the work you do will use 20 percent of your files. Seventy-five to 85 percent of documents that we retain, we never again refer to.[1]

- •Monitor the amount of paperwork and consider the time it takes to produce each document. It takes an average of fifty-four minutes to prepare a typical letter or memo; it takes almost four hours to prepare a two-and-a-quarter page report.[2] Ask yourself, "Is a written document necessary or can I make a phone call instead?"

- •If a letter, agenda, or report is necessary, use a word processor for easy updates and corrections. During breaks, take a few minutes to write a letter to your child!

- •Use previous memos and letters as standards or starting points. Sixty-five cents of every dollar spent on record-keeping is wasted on unnecessary files and duplicate copies.[3]

"Nobody ever looked back and wished they'd spent more time at work." The Colorado Tourism Board catches your eye with this statement of truth in a major magazine ad. In promoting the state of Colorado as a vacation site, the ad goes on to say, "You'll get the satisfaction of skiing the one place you've always wanted to ski. And you'll get the chance to meet some really wonderful people. Your family." What a great idea!

- •Make use of compensatory time, vacation, and personal days to rest and spend time with your family.

Use daily time-saving techniques to improve your job performance, but more importantly, use them to spend the *minimum* number of hours required of you at the job in order to spend the maximum amount of *quantity time* with your child.

Work is but one area where your time can be maximized. Let's look at some of the other areas where time-saving techniques can improve your schedule.

Chores/Errands

Chores and errands demand a great deal of time—it's the little daily jobs and tasks that seem to "bite" into your free time. Here are some helpful hints:

- Call ahead to schedule all car, appliance, and other repairs.

- Use the phone to compare prices when making major purchases.

- Keep your list of repair people up to date for emergencies.

- Pay your bills only once or twice a month.

- Make use of lunch time and breaks for trips to the bank, drugstore, cleaners, and other stops.

- Have your car repaired while you are at work.

- Use "Oil Change While You Wait" centers.

- Inquire about automatic deposit service for your paycheck and automatic checking for bill paying.

- Use an answering machine at home.

- Hire a handyperson and tradespeople to save time on painting, laundry, lawn-mowing, snow removal, and other services. Ask around for reliable people and best prices.

Completing household jobs is a necessity. This includes work on your home or apartment, automobile, and yard—the endless jobs of cleaning, upkeep, repairing, replacing, finishing, redoing, and more. How can you find time to do these things and still find time for your child? I've found three ways to tackle this situation:

- First, plan time to get a chore done without interruption by having a relative or neighbor care for your child. Plan an hour or two to dedicate yourself to the job. After that time, leave the job alone and spend good quantity time with your child.

- Second, let your child help you with chores, even if only in a small way. Here's a good rule of thumb to use when children are involved: *Estimate the time it will take you to complete the task, and multiply that by two.* For example, if you anticipate that it will take you about an hour to paint a backyard shed, realize that it will take you two hours when you involve your children. Not only does their participation slow you down, but building time into your schedule gives you a chance to take "play breaks," time to stop and see what your children are doing, and the opportunity to focus on them and not constantly on the task at hand. It gives you a break and it shows that you are interested in them and not just in getting the job done.

•A third option is to put off doing the task altogether. It is important to evaluate the chore and its significance at the present time. Could it be done at another time? Does it seem that your children are especially excited about doing something else? Is the day so beautiful that you should enjoy it with your kids? Is there an event today that you won't get another chance to attend? Sometimes I think it is helpful to use the Procrastinators Club of America's motto: "Put off 'til tomorrow everything that needn't be done today." If an opportunity to enjoy quantity time with your family comes about, grab it and be flexible! You can always complete that chore tomorrow.

Travel/Commuting

Many of us spend a considerable quantity of time traveling, whether it be by car, train, bus, or plane. Prepare for long trips and utilize other travel time for productive tasks:

•Fly nonstop whenever you can. Each time you stop or change planes, the chance for delay multiplies. Expect delays.

•When you travel by plane, make productive use of flight time.

•Use travel agents, automobile clubs, and chambers of commerce to save time when planning your trip.

•When possible, avoid rush-hour traffic to limit your waiting time on the road.

•Use cassette tapes in your car for enjoyment, learning, audio "reading," or dictating.

•When you travel by train, bring reading materials or work with you.

•When traveling, develop a reasonable, workable itinerary—don't plan either too much or too little activity for a single trip.

- Develop and use checklists—one for packing your briefcase with business materials and one for packing your suitcase with personal items and clothes. Keep a bag stocked with toiletries just for trips.

- When eating out, avoid peak meal times to limit waiting time.

- Consider bringing your family with you on business trips—particularly when you will be traveling to family-oriented destinations.

Meals

You can save time in meal preparation in order to spend more time doing other activities with your children. Or you can include them in the mealtime chores. It will probably take longer with a child helping you, but you will enjoy the time you spend together in the kitchen. Make it enjoyable. Here are some time-saving tips:

- Use appliances such as microwave or convection ovens. Microwave ovens, which are particularly useful for reheating food, can dramatically cut down on food preparation time.

- Develop a weekly meal planner by writing out the menu, the foods, and ingredients needed. This meal plan will be a time-saving guide for shopping and meal preparation.

- Whenever possible, cook casseroles and other dishes ahead of time. These make great, fast meals on evenings when time is running short.

- Try to grocery shop just once a week. Shopping for food at a crowded supermarket more often than this is time-consuming and unnecessary. You may want to check with your local market to determine their slow times.

- Evaluate the time you spend hunting for food savings. Coupons are great, but are they taking up more time than they are worth?

- Consider taking the family for an evening out. Sometimes the best thing to make for dinner is a reservation.

Other Daily Activities

Let's look at the rest of Your Ideal Week with respect to "giving the best of yourself to your family" and "making the time." Any activities in the areas of sleep, personal care, education, religious/volunteer work and leisure that focus on improving your attitude toward parenting, that help you set a good example for your child, that aid in effective time management, or meet your own needs and desires are activities that should become part of your daily schedule.

Pay close attention to sleep. The quality of your nights reflects and affects the quality of your day. Know the amount of sleep you need. There is no shortcut. Sleep is a necessity. Personal care is an area that each individual must look at. Everyone needs to keep personal hygiene a priority. Examine your schedule for time-savers.

Your interest in exercise will vary daily and should be scheduled accordingly. Today there are over 12,000 companies in the U.S. with some sort of wellness, health promotion, or fitness program. Studies demonstrate that when you exercise on a regular basis—at least three times a week for a minimum of twenty minutes each session—you become more productive.

•Schedule time for exercise before or after work.

•Ask if you can bring your child to the health club.

Many adults with families are pursuing academic degrees. Only you can determine the priority value of continuing education, and always in consultation with a partner or co-parent, if yours is a two-parent family. You should realize that furthering your education is very time-consuming and demanding. The demands of school can become a source of additional stress on you and your family relationships.

You are the one who decides how you will spend each moment of day. Try to select the activities that are most important, and keep your priorities in order as you decide how much time will be spent on each activity.

4. Minimize Time-Wasters

Waiting

There's a lot of quantity time spent waiting in our lives. Obviously, waiting time cannot be eliminated completely, so be prepared for it. Use waiting time to catch up on reading, letter writing, or even work. Bring reading materials or work to places where you might have to wait: doctors' or lawyers' offices; train, plane, or bus terminals. Instead of getting annoyed at waiting, you will have an opportunity to make good use of your time. Call ahead for appointments to minimize your waiting time.

Sometimes the Waiting Process Is Significant

I've now forgotten when I first learned to play chess, but it was when I was very young. I remember that the game appeared to be very challenging, especially with the many unique playing figures, and that it required a significant amount of time and patience by my parents to instruct me properly in the rules of the game.

Our family had a very special chess set, which had been sent to us from friends in Germany. My parents were the only ones allowed to get this set off the shelf; it was not to be handled by the children. I recall that I stayed passionately interested in chess for more than a year. And during that time, my parents almost always allotted time to play with me, even with three other children and their own diverse interests. I recall how special this time was to me, especially the waiting time between moves. Only years later, as a parent with time pressures of my own, did I realize how significant this waiting time really was.

It's hard to believe that it has already been more than seven years since I inherited this special chess set. To anyone else it may appear a somewhat ordinary set, but to me it signifies more than just a game. It's a symbol of my parents' commitment to my growth. It reminds me that I was a priority in their lives.

Television

During the past ten years, television viewing has increased to six hours and fifty-five minutes per day per average household. Adults as well as children are watching a substantial amount of television. In order to be more time efficient, a parent should limit his or her television viewing. *The Wall Street Journal* conducted a survey of CEOs of Fortune 500 companies about their leisure activities. Watching TV was not a popular activity. The CEOs reported the number of hours they watched. Eighty-one percent said they watched one hour or less per day![4]

Some families have taken a strong stand against television by removing the television set in their house. Although this transition is usually very difficult, it improves communication within the family, prompting family members to develop and enjoy other leisure interests together. Eliminating television is a drastic measure. It's obviously not for everyone. Watching selected television programs and videos can be very enjoyable and educational (see Chapter 4 for suggestions on viewing television with your child), but you need to limit the viewing time—for both you and your child.

Be more aware of the number of hours you are watching television and, of course, the types of programs. I've gotten into the habit of watching the nightly news after the children have gone to bed. And with the availability of a VCR, I now have the flexibility of spending time with Zachary, Ryan, and Sue while recording a favorite movie or sports event for viewing at a later time. (Many times I never even bother to watch the tape afterward.)

Just remember, one of the easiest ways to find more time in your day is simply to turn off the television set or the VCR. It's easy to press that "on" button, but it's hard to make the commitment to use television viewing time more productively.

"Time is the coin of your life. It is the only coin you have, and only you can determine how it will be spent. Be careful lest you let other people spend it for you."

—*Carl Sandburg*

4

Playing Is for Children . . . and for You, Too

"Every little boy (child) has inside of him an aching void which demands interesting and exciting play. And if you don't fill it with something that is interesting and exciting and good for him, he is going to fill it with something that is interesting and exciting and isn't good for him."

—*Theodore Roosevelt, Jr.*

You never quite knew when it would happen, but when it did, there were thousands of them. They were becoming a nuisance—to me, that is. Ryan and two friends, Matthew and Andrea, found them to be a treasure, an unlimited supply of fun. Fall brought a hoard of acorns dropping into our front yard. Squirrels took only so many. The rest were left for the children. They wanted them all. After collecting a few hundred, Matthew (8), Andrea (6), and Ryan (2), came into the garage. Their adventure started by putting the acorns into a variety of trucks, then dumping them in strategic spots throughout the garage and driveway. After scavenging them back up, Ryan and his friends dispensed them into containers. This inspired the children to make a table setup, which led to cooking meals, which resulted in an acorn feast! This was followed by a mass transfer of acorns to a red wagon that quickly went outside. The children returned into the garage without the acorns, ready for their next adventure. They played and played. If you looked past the garage, now in complete disarray, you could see children in action: parents' examples revealed, life-styles recreated, values displayed, emotions uncovered, motor control and dexterity exhibited, and creativity unfolding. Children at work. Play at its best.

Total involvement. Children learning. Children growing. Play provides a child with the opportunity to satisfy curiosity, build self-esteem, face challenges, have pleasurable experiences, and express the inner self.

S T A R T IS: SHAPING TOMORROW'S ADULTS BY REACHING OUT TODAY

DAY 13 : START acting as a positive catalyst for your child by providing an atmosphere of playfulness in the home. This promotes enjoyment and growth in your child and closeness between the two of you.

Play is FUNdamental

Play has been defined by many learning experts, from Freud to Piaget, from Erickson to Montessori. I define play as *voluntary participation in a safe activity for pleasure*. Play is fun. It is also the process by which a child learns about the world and grows as a unique individual.

Children acquire knowledge about the physical and social worlds in which they live through playful interaction with objects and people. Children do not need to be forced to learn; they are motivated by their own desire to make sense of their world.

A child grows physically, mentally, emotionally, and socially through such activities as arts, crafts, dance, drama, hobbies, music, outdoor activities, and sports. And every child needs a variety of experiences that will develop distinct characteristics and personality traits. Arts and crafts activities develop creativity and artistic skills, helping a child become more confident, feel a sense of accomplishment, and appreciate and understand the concepts of design, color, and form. Sports develop strength and motor skills, helping a child become more fit, more physically skilled and, hopefully, a good sport and better team player. Play develops many areas of the personality, and one set of traits is no less important than the others.

Through play children *learn* cooperation, problem-solving techniques, self-reliance, sharing, team play, and the significance of rules and order. Children *gain* knowledge in language, math, science, art, music, nature, dance, and physical fitness, not only in a typical classroom setting but also through their voluntary involvement in recreational activities. Play also helps children *develop* curiosity, confidence, strength, motor skills, coordination, values, imagination, judgment, freedom of expression, concentration, musical aptitude, and an appreciation for the outdoors. During playtimes they *acquire* creativity, the ability to choose between alternatives, self-direction, dexterity, flexibility, and artistic and musical talents. Most important, play helps children acquire a stronger belief in themselves and an awareness of what provides pleasure for them now and for the future.

For your child the importance of play lies both in how they participate (the process) and the accomplishment (the product).

Adults tend to view play as a means to an end, whereas your child will ignore the end in order to explore, enjoy, and toy with the means (Fagan, 1984).[1]

To a young child, the *result* of the play activity is secondary. As adults, our orientation and respect is tied up in the end product.[2] Until the ages of seven or eight, your child will be much more interested in what he or she is doing (the process) rather than how play turns out (the product).[3] As the old saying so aptly puts it, "I (the child) don't want a threaded needle, I want to thread a needle." Think of this when your child is playing. "I don't want a sand castle built, I want to build a sand castle." Or "I don't want a cooked meal (pretend play), I want to cook a meal." And ever so important is, "I don't want a colored picture, I want to color a picture."

A child under the age of eight participates and perceives the playtime activity for the process. Your child sees play for its FACE value, quickly evaluating any activity by asking, "Is it Fun, Active, Challenging, or Exciting?" If it meets the FACE standards, your child is bound to participate. The finished product, if there is one, is just an added bonus.

Knowing that children value the "process" more than the "product" should influence your approach to everyday tasks. When you are dressing your child or asking her or him to clean a bedroom, your child will ask unconsciously, "Will this be fun?" On the other hand, you as the adult, are more interested in the finished product. If you try to make the task more appealing and fun—more like play—the job will get done more quickly and with less stress! You are not "giving in." On the contrary, you are understanding and meeting your child's play-time needs while also achieving your goals and requests.

Children of different ages relate to the same activity in different ways. Look for evidence of this during any holiday season, especially Christmas, Hanukkah, or Kwanza. Preschoolers become very excited when their family begins to unpack the holiday decorations, unearthing the "treasures of the past." They can hold and play with the holiday trimmings and ornaments and watch the colored lights. It's a stimulating process of discovery that engages all a child's senses—but only for a short period of time. As your child grows older (age five to seven), he or she takes more time inspecting the holiday decorations, examining and exploring each and every item. Older children (age eight and above) have a more sophisticated and purposeful interest in the holiday paraphernalia. He or she may develop and construct a nativity scene, decorate a room or tree, bake a batch of cookies, or create an outdoor light display. The physical outcome of these activities may not meet his parent's preconceived notions of what, for example, a Nativity scene *should* look like, but the finished product will have significant meaning to the child. Give your child positive feedback no matter what his or her age and no matter what the finished product.

Play Is Work; Work Is Play

Children do not differentiate between play, learning, and work. This is easily apparent in a child's desire to help with adult tasks and chores. It is also mirrored in the toy industry and the popularity of children's "let's pretend" toys.

Your child's innate interest in virtually everything provides an opportunity to involve him or her in your task. Now you may say, "But it's too complex," or "It's too dangerous," or "My child will not be interested." This is the wrong attitude. Household jobs, if presented correctly, look like play to children. It seems like fun to wash the dishes—just look at all those bubbles in the water—and help out with dusting, vacuuming, and meal preparation. Your child will also enjoy participating in outside work such as mowing the lawn, raking, or painting. Working with a child now will help develop positive attitudes toward doing these tasks, which will later become known as work, chores, or jobs. Simple things such as starting the vacuum cleaner, mixing the paint, or filling a wheelbarrow with leaves become important to your child. He or she is helping you and participating in your world. Your child should be praised for helping out. As children mature, you will be pleased when they are willing to do these jobs on their own. The most important foundation for a child's healthy development is the reciprocally pleasurable play between adults and children. Cladwell stated that "playful play is related to all things that we want young children to learn to do."[4]

The learning and the information that children retain is influenced by many stimuli. A child's development is a complex integration of heredity and environment. The sex of your child, social and ethnic backgrounds, parent-child and teacher-child interactions, sibling and peer influences, physical environment, television, and books are continuously contributing to your child's maturation. Be aware of these influences, but most of all, be a major factor in your child's life.

$ T A R T IS: Shaping Tomorrow's Adults by Reaching Out Today

DAY 14 : START introducing your child to various activities from the "Six Activity Groups." This generates a well-balanced menu of interests and options.

What's Your Activity Diet Look Like?

The importance of play, your child's expanding interests, and your desire to participate with your child will bring about the need to explore a wide variety of activities.

In working with children and adults, I have enjoyed participating in and teaching many recreational or leisure activities. These fall into Six Main Groups: arts and crafts, dance and drama, hobbies, music, outdoor activities, and sports and games. As children grow, it is essential that they get to explore and develop interests. In fact, the more interests they have, the easier it will be for them to occupy and enjoy their time. We all have been taught to eat a balanced diet, one that consists of the basic food groups. Similarly, when you expose your child to activities from each of the Six Activity Groups, you aid in the development of his or her social, mental, and physical well-being.

The following questionnaire invites you to look at your interests. By recognizing what it is that holds your attention, you will have a clearer idea where you are directing your child. From this Interest Inventory you will be able to tell whether or not you are offering your child a "balanced activity diet."

The following list is an inventory of 150 activities divided into the six groups. Using the indicated number scale, rate your frequency of participation for each activity. If a particular activity is not listed, write this activity in the space labeled "Other" for the proper category, then give your frequency rating. Total your rating points in the areas provided and rank the group from high to low.

Interest Inventory

For the following 150 activities, rate your frequency of participation in the activity. The ratings are:

3   Participate at least once a week
2   Participate occasionally, about once a month
1   Participate in three or four times a year
0   Do not participate at all

After completing each the inventory for each activity group, total all the points in each category.

ART and CRAFTS

____ Cake decorating

____ Candle making

____ Cartooning

____ Ceramics

____ Clothes design

____ Flower arts

____ Interior design

____ Jewelry design

____ Kite making

____ Knitting and other hand work

____ Leather work

____ Metal work

____ Native lore

____ Origami

____ Quilting

____ Painting/Water color

____ Papier-mache

____ Sculpture

____ Sewing

____ Sketching

____ Visiting art galleries

____ Visiting museums

____ Weaving

____ Woodworking

____Other_____

_____TOTAL POINTS

DANCE and DRAMA

____ Acting in plays

____ Aerobics

____ Ballet

____ Ballroom dancing

____ Carnivals/Circuses

____ Cheerleading/Twirling

____ Clowning

____ Dancing (social, square, etc.))

____ Doll collecting

____ Drama (acting, makeup, lighting, etc.)

____ Fashion modeling

____ Folk dancing

____ Gymnastics

____ Jazzercise

____ Mime and movement

____ Movie attendance

____ Pageants (talent, beauty)

____ Public speaking

____ Puppetry

____ Rope skipping/Double Dutch

____ Storytelling

____ Tap

____ Theater attendance

____ Yoga

____Other_____

_____TOTAL POINTS

HOBBIES

____ Antiques/Furniture restoration

____ Appliance repair

____ Auto mechanics or restoration

____ Coin collecting

____ Computer programming

____ Cooking

____ Electronics

____ First aid

____ "Flea marketing"

____ Indoor gardening

____ Model building

____ Model railroads

____ Pet training/Shows

____ Photography

____ Puzzles

____ Reading

____ Rock Collecting

____ Rocketry

____ Shell collecting

____ Sports card collecting

____ Stamp collecting

____ Video making

____ Word games/crossword puzzles

____ Writing (poetry, books, etc)

____Other_____

_____TOTAL POINTS

MUSIC

____ Accordion

____ Banjo

____ Caroling

____ Chorus/Choir

____ Collecting music memorabilia

____ Concert attendance

____ Conducting

____ Drum

____ Flute

____ Guitar

____ Harmonica or kazoo

____ Listening to recorded music

____ Music composition

____ Opera attendance

____ Organ

____ Piano

____ Parade participant or spectator

____ Playing an instrument

(other than listed here)

____ Playing in a band

____ Saxophone

____ Singing in a band

____ Trumpet

____ Violin

____ Voice training

____ Other_____

_____TOTAL POINTS

OUTDOOR ACTIVITIES

____ Archery

____ Astronomy

____ Bicycling

____ Bird-watching

____ Boating

____ Camping

____ Climbing

____ Environmental cleanup/recycling

____ Fishing

____ Gardening

____ Hiking

____ Horseback riding

____ Hunting/trapping

____ Jogging

____ Kite flying

____ Lawn games (bocce, croquet, Frisbee, horsehoe, etc.)

____ Orienteering

____ Picnicing

____ Recreational vehicle riding

____ Riflery (skeet, trapshooting)

____ Skateboarding

____ Skiing (downhill, cross-country)

____ Walking

____ Water sports (skating, skiing, sledding, etc.)

____ Other_____

_____TOTAL POINTS

SPORTS/GAMES

____ Basketball

____ Billiards

____ Bowling

____ Boxing/wrestling

____ Cards/board games

____ Computer/video games

____ Darts

____ Fencing

____ Field sports (baseball, football, softball, soccer

____ Gaming/gambling

____ Golf

____ Gymnastics

____ Handball

____ Hockey (field, ice, street)

____ Lacrosse

____ Martial arts

____ Racquet sports (badminton, tennis, racquetball, squash, platform tennis

____ Skating (ice, in-line, roller)

____ Swimming/diving

____ Table Tennis

____ Track/field

____ Vehicle racing

____ Volleyball

____ Weightlifting

____ Other_____

_____TOTAL POINTS

List the total points for each category below:

_____ Arts and Crafts
_____ Dance and Drama
_____ Hobbies
_____ Music
_____ Outdoor Activities
_____ Sports and Games

List the activity groups in high(1) to low (6) order from the list above:

1._____
2._____
3._____
4._____
5._____
6._____

These Are a Few of My Favorite Things

During your child's early development, you can play a major role in introducing him or her to a wide variety of activities. The more activities your child becomes familiar with, the more options your child can select from as he or she develops. It would be wonderful if your child likes the same activities as you, but don't expect that. It is important and necessary for your child to develop his or her own interests.

After taking the Interest Inventory, you know what your major interests are, what you like to do, and what activities you feel comfortable exposing your child to. Introducing your child to your favorite activities will benefit both of you greatly. Your child will sense the pleasure you receive from a given activity and will be intrigued with and interested in it for that reason alone.

And you will be able to share your enthusiasm and excitement! Your positive, fun-filled attitude will be contagious as you and your child enjoy activities together.

What about the last three categories in your Interest Inventory (the ones ranked 4, 5, and 6), those activity groups in which you have a minimal amount of skill or experience? This is where opportunities open up for you. Become involved in a new activity from one of these lower-ranked groups. Take a class—try something new on your own, do it with a friend or neighbor and, of course, do it with your child. You both will be learning something new and sharing a special experience. It's important for your child to see you being open to different activities, possibly failing but seeing that you are trying and doing your best. Children need to realize that parents are not perfect and can be open to learning new skills. They will mirror your willingness to learn.

If you have no interest in a particular activity but would like your child to be exposed it, look for ways your child can participate. YMCAs, town recreation programs, libraries, friends, relatives, churches, and school programs offer many activities for children. Regardless of your interest, be sure to provide positive feedback on your child's interest and continued enjoyment in an activity. (Hopefully, your child will persuade you to become interested in participating.) Remember, your child is a unique individual, and his or her interests will be a combination of some interests that you might share and others in which your only involvement will be complete and enthusiastic support. You don't have to be interested in participating in all your child's activities, but make sure you're interested in your child!

Going the Extra Mile

You may want to ask your partner (if you have one) or child, depending on the child's age, to fill out the activities on the Interest Inventory and compare your lists. Use the inventory list as a starting point for new playtime ideas or gift selections.

Guidelines:

- Do not be judgmental about your partner's or child's selections.

- Do not use gifts as a substitute for your own participation and involvement.

- Do not force activities or interests on your child.

DAY 15 : START making your child's environment stimulating, interesting, stable, enjoyable, and safe. A positive environment provides the right setting for your child's inherited characteristics to develop to the fullest.

Characteristics of Children: Ages and Stages

Parents whose children have grown to be adults always share the same insight with new parents: "Enjoy your children now because they grow up so fast." Trust that this statement is true and take the quantity time today to observe and be a part of your child's development and world of play.

Every child is special, but a majority of children go through various developmental sequences and stages that are similar. It is exciting and fascinating for parents to watch their children's emotions, skills, and confidence mature at each developmental stage. Here is a brief synopsis of "average" skills and developmental milestones at various ages, and suggested playthings for children in each age group, and a few parenting tips.

Age: 0-6 Months

Skills or capabilities:

Supports head in prone position

Loses grasping reflex

Crying replaced with nodding, smiling, babbling, and cooing

Follows moving person or object with eyes

Sits without being propped

Babbling stage

Starts to reach and grasp for objects

Rolls over both ways

Explores hands and feet; puts objects in mouth

Toys/learning tools: Mobiles, rattles, teethers, squeeze toys, keys on ring, crib gyms, soft dolls or small plush animals, mirror (unbreakable and fastened to crib, playpen, or wall), brightly patterned crib sheets, pictures near crib, music box or mobile, and, most important, *parents*.

Tips for parents: It's a special time, a new beginning for both parent and baby, and a fresh awareness for life and its amazing development. Become absorbed in your baby's daily changes and growth.

Age: 7-12 Months

Skills or capabilities:

Begins to sit alone; crawls; starts to walk

Stands alone for short time

Knows name

Imitates motions such as claps, waves, pattycakes, "so big"

Exhibits stranger anxiety

Imitates sound sequences; utters first words; understands simple words

Climbs, rolls, or throws ball

Puts objects into and out of things

Enjoys stories; begins to show interest in picture books

With objects wants to: bang, insert, poke, twist, squeeze, drop, shake, bite, throw, open/shut, push/pull, empty/fill, or drag along

Toys/learning tools: Pots and pans, soft blocks, simple floating toys, soft hand puppets, books (cloth, plastic, or cardboard), infant swing (used with adult supervision), dolls, large balls, shake/rattle/squeak/musical toys, large plastic vehicles

Tips for parents: Communication and mobility become a reality for your child. Child-proof your home for peace of mind. Be your child's guide to seeing more of the world, both indoors and outdoors.

Age: 1-2 Years

Skills or capabilities:

Pushes, pulls objects

Starts using fork and spoon to eat

Stacks two to three objects

Knows parts of the face

Gives and takes toys

Likes to climb

Shows great curiosity

Enjoys water and sand play

Begins imitative play in caretaking and housekeeping tasks

Relates to adults better than to children

Starts with one word "talk" progressing to two and three words (may know from fifty to seventy-five words)

Toys/learning tools: Stable four-wheel ride-ons, wooden blocks, simple puzzles with knobs, shape sorters, tunnels, toy telephone, sandbox, pool, surprise box, large crayons for scribbling, slide, pull toys, bean bags, books with familiar objects and bright colors, learning or dressing dolls

Tips for parents: Your child has developed a visible personality. Relating to your child brings about a variety of responses. Stimulate conversation with your child and share as much of yourself as you can.

Age: 2-3 Years

Skills or capabilities:

Runs, stands and sits

Speaks three- to four-word sequences

Frequently asks, "What's that?" and "Why?"

Stacks five to six blocks

Starts toilet training or is toilet trained

Has a short attention span; tires easily

Is easily frustrated

Throws and retrieves balls

Develops counting skills

Enjoys fantasy and make-believe play

Starts to play with other children

Toys/learning tools: Wagons, carriages, child-size wheelbarrow, toy lawnmower, toy vacuum, shopping cart, tricycle, climbing structures, magnetic board (with letters, numbers, and animals), balls, sled, pounding and hammering toys, tub toys, all instruments, horns and whistles, paints, blunt scissors, construction paper, chalkboard, toy cars, trucks and trains, play dough, regular crayons, puzzles, dolls, books with concepts (letters, numbers, spatial concepts)

Tips for parents: Energy and curiosity abound at this age. Focus not on where it all comes from but on how to channel those forces into the right direction. Your child's feelings are beginning to surface, positively and negatively, but your child's "two's" do not have to be "terrible." Provide constant stimulation and feedback that builds confidence.

Age: 3-5 Years (Preschool)

Skills or capabilities:
Enjoys climbing, jumping, skipping, and dancing
Likes to imitate and dramatize
Is creative with hands; enjoys art and building things
Enjoys music and simple colors
Likes to pretend
Shows ability for socialization; able to interact with peers
Has a longer attention span
Reveals feelings in dramatic play
Shows interest in producing designs
Demonstrates peak interest in dramatic play
Displays limited coordination, with motor skills unevenly
    developed

Toys/learning tools: Simple board games, books with colorful pictures and short texts, small bicycle with training wheels, balance beam (low), puzzles of twenty to fifty pieces (depending on age), ice skates, roller skates, play sets (including doll house, farm, garage, airport, space, forts), housekeeping and storekeeping toys, flannel board with pictures and letters, glue or paste, tunnel of fun, hardware tools, Legos or any construction toys, wooden alphabet and numbers

Tips for parents: Imagination, dramatization, and explicit imitation of adult examples surface. Your child can now place earlier discoveries in a more realistic context. The world is starting to really make sense. Be a positive pillar in your child's world.

Age: 6-8 Years

Skills or capabilities:

Likes games of chance and skill

Still enjoys housekeeping toys

Displays a hunger for exercise

Displays a prominent tendency for fighting

Is imitative, especially of adults

Is eager for attention

Likes to show off, hold center of the stage; wants to win

Has no concept of time

Is curious about people and the world

Develops an ability to learn to play real instruments and read music

Shows interest in formal dance lessons

Shows interest in nature and science

Likes to collect things

Likes magic

Toys/learning tools: More complex climbing structures, map puzzles, sports equipment, strategy and rules games, science and model kits, simple typewriter, electric trains, craft kits for jewelry and leather work, tape or CD player, jump ropes, books of all kinds including book and tape combinations

Tips for parents: Your child has gained much more control of her or his behavior, but there is also much bottled-up enthusiasm waiting to be released. Pull the plug for excitement and fun. Be a catalyst by promoting ongoing learning in the world surrounding your child.

Age: 9-12 Years

Skills or capabilities:

Engages in active play, team efforts, and development of sports skills

Starts hobbies; builds collections

Enjoys games that stress strategy and develop knowledge

Demonstrates a desire for adventure, exploration

Becomes more concerned with personal appearance

Enters "hero worship" stage

Wants to learn by experience

Enjoys constructing things

Wants to be part of a group

Likes rewards—points, stars, badges

Likes to store facts, classify and identify information

Resists being told what to do

Develops good attention span; can be passive spectator; enjoys
    competitive games and sports

Demonstrates growing interest in community and the world

May develop particular interest in a type of animal

Toys/learning tools: Checkers or chess, handicrafts sets, model kits,
jigsaw puzzles, makeup and grooming kits, paint sets, outdoor sport
equipment, bicycle, roller skates/in-line skates, ice skates, scrapbooks,
music (tapes or CDs), computers and educational software programs,
simple biographies, chapter books with less pictures and more text

Tips for parents: Your child is growing up and wants to be treated
like an adult, but she or he still needs a bountiful supply of patience
and love. Your child is willing to be challenged and is establishing and
accomplishing individual and team goals. Be a strong supporter.

Help Your Child Enjoy a Smorgasbord

As your child progresses through the various developmental stages,
try acquainting her or him with the Six Activity Groups. What would
I recommend to give your child a well-rounded experience with the
activities in each group? Let's look at the Big Picture of a developing
child and the playthings and opportunities that can continue to provide
knowledge, skills, and enjoyment as your child grows. Here's a check-
list for you:

Arts and Crafts

___ Crayons, construction paper, paint, paste, and scissors

___ Modeling dough—clay or play dough

___ Table with chairs (child-size)

___ Chalkboard or white board and easel

___ Opportunities to create an "art masterpiece" in any form

Dance and Drama

___ Children's videos

___ Tools, dishes, etc.

___ Dolls, stuffed animals, puppets

___ Boxes of all sizes

___ Opportunities to attend or be in plays and dances

Hobbies

___ A library card

___ Puzzles, board games

___ Blocks, construction sets

___ Access to a computer at home, at school, or at the library

___ Opportunities to collect things

Music

___ Instruments—bought or homemade

___ Tape or CD player

___ Songs to sing

___ Music lessons

___ Opportunities to attend concerts and musical shows

Outdoor Activities

___ Sandbox and small pool

___ Park to visit

___ Playhouse, tent, or fort

___ Riding toys, including a bike

___ Endless opportunities to jump, run, skip, and hop

Sports and Games

___ Balls

___ Racquets, golf clubs, and bats

___ Climbing apparatus/playground equipment

___ Bowling set

___ Opportunity to be on sports teams

Toys, of course, are among the major "tools of play." Toy Manufacturers of America, Inc., the trade association for U.S. producers and importers of playthings and holiday decorations, categorize playthings into fourteen basic types:

1. Balls
2. Dolls
3. Stuffed toys
4. Construction toys—toys to stack, assemble, and build
5. "Let's pretend" toys—children's replicas of adult items
6. Self-expression toys—instruments for creativity
7. Music and rhythm toys
8. Things to climb—apparatus to develop gross motor skills
9. Junior sports equipment—scaled-down versions of regular sports equipment
10. Vehicles—transportation in all sizes
11. Mechanical/electrical and battery-operated toys
12. Games—skill, board, card, and strategy games
13. New Technology Games—computer, VCRs, and learning aids
14. Hobbies and crafts—kit forms for all skills and interests

When looking through any toy store, you will realize two things. There is an unlimited selection of playthings for each of the fourteen toy categories. The second observation is that playthings have become very costly. The world of technology and electronics has produced sophisticated toys such as talking/walking/crying dolls, child-sized motorized cars, remote control cars, boats, and airplanes and, of course, Nintendo and other TV computer games. These toys can be very enjoyable for your child, but only if you wish to make a cash outlay that easily exceeds $100. There are less costly alternatives that yield a much more intimate play partnership between you and your child.

Two Years of Fun for 69¢

Two years ago I bought a toy for 69¢ and we are still enjoying it today. The toy is a brown, sixteen-inch, inflatable football that Sue and I bought at the local five-and-dime drugstore. Most towns still have at least one shop that offers playthings for under $1.00—yes, one dollar. The football has survived being thrown and kicked through leaf piles in fall, heavy snowdrifts in winter, mud puddles in early spring, and wading pool water in summer. When the football needed a new valve, we improvised with part of a golf tee. Quite a toy for 69¢, plus tax!

With some hunting for a five-and-dime store and some creativity, you can find a wide variety of surprisingly great playthings for you and your child to enjoy together. Here are suggestions for a multitude of activities that can be enjoyed for under $1.00:

•Make a "schmerltz" by placing a tennis ball in an old athletic sock and tying a knot in the sock above the ball. It's now ready to be thrown back and forth and caught by its tail.

•Take a roll of kite string or yarn and "yard weave" or "room weave" by wrapping the string around items indoors or outdoors. Once you've created your "spider web," hang objects on it for an amusing effect. The final task is cutting it all down, an adventure in itself.

•A bag of balloons provides cool relief in the summertime when you transform it into a bag of water bombs.

•In winter, balloons can be used indoors for volleyball games or used with rolled newspaper bats for an informal, make-your-own-rules game of baseball or tennis.

•A beach ball provides hours of outdoor fun in the summer or indoor fun in the winter (in a garage, basement, or playroom).

•Create artistic masterpieces with a small watercolor set, crayons, blank paper, or a coloring book.

•Colored chalk can be used on paper or outdoors on sidewalks and driveways (it easily washes off).

•A long piece of rope instantly lets a number of people jump rope together, or it can be cut into many jump ropes so each person can have their own.

•Plastic kickballs, usually priced at 99¢, have endless possibilities, including the game of kickball, soccer, or spud.

- A blank cassette tape (along with a tape player, which can be borrowed if you do not have one) gives you and your child the freedom to sing songs, tell stories, or become radio announcers.

- Use rolls of masking tape, pieces of cardboard, a ruler, a pencil, blank envelopes, and picture stamps to have your child set up a make-believe post office.

- A pack of blank paper along with a library book on origami will help you and your child create paper masterpieces beyond the normal airplanes and hats.

- Jacks and a ball remain a favorite childhood toy.

- Marbles offer as much fun now as they ever did. Marbles can be combined ingeniously with old pipes and paraphernalia from the garage or attic to make an original "Mouse Trap" game.

- A deck of playing cards provides an unlimited amount of card games for all age levels, and these are all great quiet activities. Popular card games such as "Old Maid" or "Go Fish" may also be purchased in special card packs.

- Pick-up sticks always challenges a child!

- A pack of stick-on letters and numbers and some paper or cardboard is great for creating signs, cards, or posters.

- During Easter buy an extra package of plastic eggs for hiding mini-surprises or candy. You can have an egg hunt any time of the year.

- Purchase a blank writing book or diary for writing stories or drawing pictures.

- Other great supplies for adult/child activities include a package of popsicle or craft sticks and glue for building; construction paper and scissors for many paper craft projects; a package of beads, string, and dry pasta shapes to make charming bracelets and necklaces; pipe cleaners to create stick figures and animals; newspapers and magazines for scrapbook cut-outs.

- Buy a bottle of bubble soap to blow outdoors or in the bathtub.

- Turn old socks, decorated with cloth scraps and buttons, into puppets.

•A package of stencils can be used for unlimited drawing.

•Use a bucket of water and a paint brush to "paint" the exterior your house, or if you have wood scraps and some old house paint, your child can really paint.

•For painting indoors, use sponges with any type of paint for sponge painting.

•Combine a flute, whistle, or kazoo along with a homemade drum for a parade or band.

•Use a Super Ball for outdoor games or a Nerf ball for indoor play.

•Collect ordinary kitchen ingredients to make homemade modeling dough using the following recipe (remember, stove-top cooking projects are only for adults or adult-supervised older children):

1 cup flour	1/2 cup salt
2 teaspoons cream of tartar	1 cup water
1 tablespoon salad oil	Food coloring to tint

Mix all of the ingredients in a saucepan. Cook over low heat, stirring constantly, until a ball forms and pulls away from the sides of the pan. Remove the ball to a cutting board and allow it to cool. When cool, knead the dough until soft. Place the modeling dough in an air-tight food storage bag or container so it can be used again and again.

•A cookie or cake mix makes an easy baking project. If you don't have a mix, try this recipe for making pretzels:

1 package dry yeast	1 tablespoon sugar
1 1/2 cups warm water	4 cups flour
1 teaspoon salt	1 egg yolk

Mix together the yeast with warm water. Add the salt, sugar, and flour. Knead the dough until it is soft. Divide the dough into pieces and your child can roll them into shapes. Before baking, brush the tops and sides of the shapes with egg yolk. Bake on a cookie sheet for 8 to 10 minutes and "until the pretzels brown" at 425°.

•A collection of acorns, pine cones, and rocks with glue or paint create a nifty craft project.

- A package of large paper plates can make masks, clocks, and flying saucers.

- Small pieces of cloth and a package of beans can be sewn together to make bean bags.

- A package of seeds, dirt from outside, and an old milk carton or pot can start you off on some indoor gardening.

- A map of the United States placed on cardboard and carefully cut out makes a challenging and educational puzzle.

- A wiffle ball and a broom handle make a safe baseball game.

- Save your empty boxes or cans to start a hobby of collecting coins, stamps, paper clips, buttons, erasers—or anything else.

These activities are fun for any adult and child. Essentially all that is needed are some of the ordinary items mentioned above and your combined efforts. The best part is that there is no "right" way to do each activity, no time limit, and no sophisticated equipment. All each activity needs is your active participation, your overwhelming enthusiasm, and one dollar!

Old-Time Favorites

Most children receive their favorite plaything for Christmas or birthday without their parents even realizing it. It's not the store-bought doll, truck, game, or even the bike. It's a *box*! Doesn't it always seem as if the packing box is the item children play with the longest? Boxes are one of the thirteen most intriguing, absorbing, and enthralling non-toy articles children are attracted to. These articles seem to provide children with an endless amount of enjoyment and unlimited opportunities to use their imagination. Here is the entire Top Thirteen Non-Toy Favorites list:

1. Boxes	8. Buttons
2. Pots and pans	9. Styrofoam peanuts
3. Water	10. Pieces of scrap wood
4. Sand	11. String
5. Mud	12. Tape, and
6. Sawdust	13. Rubber bands
7. Blankets	

These are not toys as such, but your child will never notice the difference!

Tools for Learning

It is important to select appropriate toys for your child. Here are some helpful guidelines for choosing playthings, not only to stimulate learning but also for long-lasting enjoyment.

Toys should:

•Suit your child's age level (so consider a toy's age recommendations).

•Provide your child with opportunities to learn, discover, and explore.

•Be lasting, both in terms of durability and interest as your child grows up.

•Foster creativity.

•Encourage decision-making.

•Provide opportunities for parent-child interaction.

•Meet all of your child's developing needs—intellectual, physical, emotional, and social.

•Provide enjoyment and pleasure.

•Offer a variety of play possibilities.

•Be *safe*.

Accidents Can Be Prevented

It is important that your child has time to play, time to participate in appropriate activities with appropriate playthings, but your child also needs a safe play environment. According to U.S. Consumer Product Safety Commission estimates, each year an average of 90,000 children age fifteen or younger each year receive hospital emergency room treatment for injuries from dolls, toy trucks and cars, toy wagons, balls, and other toys.[5] To safeguard against possible injury to your child, here are some important safety considerations. Toys should:

- •NOT have sharp glass or metal edges.

- •NOT contain small parts that could become lodged in a child's windpipe, ears, or nose.

- •NOT produce loud noises or sounds that can damage hearing.

- •NOT have long strings or cords where infants and very young children can become entangled.

- •NOT have sharp points that can cut or stab children.

- •NOT be able to propel objects that could cause severe eye injuries.

- •NOT be used if electric toys have frayed or loose wires.

- •NOT be placed in a toy chest that has a free-falling lid.

- •NOT be left out in the rain or dew, as that can result in rust or damage—in many cases, this can create safety hazards.

- •NOT be used if damaged.

The U.S. Consumer Product Safety Commission offers free literature on a variety of play articles. Call 1-800-638-2772 (1-800-492-8363 for Maryland residents only) and you will hear messages with detailed information on their booklets and pamphlets. Two excellent pieces of literature are "Which Toy for Which Child—Ages Birth through Five" and "Which Toy for Which Child—Ages Six through Twelve."

The TV and the VCR

Parents must realize that TV has become part of the American lifestyle. More than 88 million households have at least one television. Almost 59 percent of households have a VCR, and the trend indicates that the percentage of households will continue to increase.

The National Institute of Education studied the effects of TV viewing on children. Six or more hours of TV viewing per day is consistently and strongly related to lower reading proficiency for children in three age groups (nine-, thirteen-, and seventeen-year-olds).[6] Besides the powerful attraction of TV, the VCR entices children to place themselves in front of the set even longer periods of time. It is also estimated that by age eighteen, a child will have seen 18,000 murders on TV, not to mention countless acts of violence. Children also are faced with a multitude of commercials. During every hour of TV programming, approximately thirteen minutes will be commercials. The average child may see up to 50,000 TV commercials each year.

But your child can benefit from TV, with your assistance. Survey results indicate that the amount of viewing that children do *with adults* makes a difference in how well children understand what is viewed.[7]

In 1974 Gordon Graves Leifer suggested that the presence of a respected adult during program viewing can greatly influence a child's reaction to the content.[8] This adult can guide the child in choosing which program to watch, clarify confusing situations during viewing, comment on what they watch, and impart positive values through interpretations of the program. Most importantly, the adult can help the child discern what is real and what is pretend.

If TV viewing is allowed in your house:

- Try to avoid placing a TV set in your child's room.

- Try to help your child select the programs.

- Monitor the number of hours your child is viewing television.

- Position "TV aids" near the TV—a globe, a dictionary, reference books, etc.—that will help answer your child's viewing questions.

As with TV, you should try to view most video programs *with* your child. Some adults ill-advisedly use the VCR as another electronic baby-sitter.

I became aware of how attracted children are to videos simply by observing my children at home, but I didn't realize their hypnotic effect until days after we returned home from a Florida vacation. While in Florida, I had rented a video camera for two days to capture our vacation on tape. It was extremely exciting to view it when we returned home (and also give a copy to the grandparents as a souvenir). But I was disappointed when this two-hour video became almost an obsession for Ryan. He begged to watch it over and over and over again. Sure, I was pleased that he was enjoying and reliving the vacation, but it was more *insidious* than that. He wanted it on just for the sake of having it on, and it ended up stifling his communication with the rest of the family. The lesson we all learned was to limit "VCR time."

VCRs, like TV, can be educational, and they do provide some quiet time. Programs and viewing times, however, should be supervised by parents. Take the *quantity time* necessary to show interest in what your child is viewing. Assist your child with selections at video rental stores and when recording shows at home. Video clubs are also available and they can provide wholesome, educational shows. Enjoy TV and VCR viewing times together, but remember the many alternatives to TV.

Reading

There is no question that most children do slow down and eventually need some quiet time. Although TV is usually the first activity to fill the quiet time void, there are many wonderful alternatives. If you are an enthusiastic reader, you will want to stimulate your child's interest in reading. Make reading time enjoyable by reading aloud, no matter what your child's age, and selecting books that will stimulate his or her interest.

Studies clearly show the educational benefits of reading for your child. Here are some excerpts from key studies, coupled with helpful reading enhancement tips.

"The influence of home environment is apparent in that students from homes with an abundance of reading materials are substantially better readers than those with few materials." [9]

•Keep reading materials in easily accessible areas, including your child's room, the family room, and even the car.

•Allow your child to tear out pictures and articles from old magazines for collages or scrapbooks.

"The best way for parents to help their children become better readers is to read to them—even when they are very young. Children benefit most from reading aloud when they discuss stories, learn to identify letters and words, and talk about the meaning of words."10

•Go to the library with your child and help him or her choose books. Libraries also offer a variety of children's programs like story hours, that you can enjoy together.

•Read to your child at bedtime.

"Children improve their reading ability by reading a lot. Reading achievement is directly related to the amount of reading children do in school and outside." 11

•Read all printed matter available—magazines, signs, junk mail, even the backs of cereal boxes—with your child.

•Enroll your child in a monthly book club or buy a subscription to a magazine that will hold his or her interest.

There are many children's book clubs. Magazines such as *Parents*, *Family Life*, *Parenting*, or *Family Fun* offer many advertisements for book clubs aimed at a variety of ages and interests. There are an estimated 11,000 consumer, trade, academic, literary, and single-subject magazines published in the U.S. alone.

An excellent magazine for younger children (ages two to six) and their parents is *Sesame Street Magazine* published by the Children's Television Workshop (CTW). Not only does your child get a magazine each month, but parents also receive an informational supplement. CTW also publishes *Kid City Magazine* for ages six to ten and *3-2-1 Contact* for ages eight to fourteen. Other popular magazines include *Highlights for Children* for ages two to twelve; *Sports Illustrated for Kids*; the National Geographic Society's *World* for children age eight and older; the National Wildlife Federation's *Your Big Backyard* for ages three to five and *Ranger Rick* for ages six to twelve; the Children's

Better Health Institute's *Humpty Dumpty* for ages four to six, *Jack and Jill* for ages seven to nine and *Children's Digest* for ages ten to twelve; *Faces: The Magazine about People* for ages eight to fourteen; Boy Scouts of America's *Boy's Life*; Girl Scouts of the U.S.A.'s *American Girl*; and *Stone Soup*, a literary magazine of writings and art from children ages six to twelve.

"Telling young children stories can motivate them to read. Storytelling also introduces them to cultural values and literary traditions before they can read, write, and talk about stories themselves." [12]

•Listen to story cassettes on long trips in the car.

•Schedule a quiet time for the whole family to read, a time to read a book together out loud, or a time for each family member to become involved with his or her own book.

Of course, there are many other quiet alternatives to TV, including card or board games, puzzles, recorded music, craft kits, art projects, and computer games and educational/entertainment software.

A Word about Computers

Computers have become a part of everyone's life in some fashion. They are both learning tools and entertainment centers. Many adults have to take computer literacy courses to catch up with the latest technology, and children are being exposed to computers at school and in the homes of their playmates. Almost 95 percent of all U.S. schools have computers. According to the Software Publishers Association, some 27percent of America's nine million households now have personal computers. Here are some parenting tips on computer technology:

•Your child should become knowledgeable and proficient in the use of computers because *computers are here to stay*. When should kids learn about computers? A survey of 135,208 children conducted by General Mills tells us an early start is in order. Fifty-four percent said they thought computer instruction should begin in elementary school, 40 percent said in kindergarten, and 6 percent said junior high school.

• Technology (hardware) and program selection (software) are advancing at a rapid rate. Try to keep up with what is happening by reading relevant articles, finding out what your child is using at school, and visiting computer stores.

• If you are uncomfortable with computers, take a short computer course or receive instructions from a knowledgeable relative or friend. I also suggest you ask your child to help you master the computer or a specific software program—it is excellent togetherness time and it boosts your child's self-esteem. Your interest in the capabilities of computers will help your child's school work.

• A computer can be an excellent learning tool or an expensive plaything. It's up to you to help your child decide how it will be used. There's room for both the learning and pure fun experiences.

S T A R T IS: SHAPING TOMORROW'S ADULTS BY REACHING OUT TODAY

DAY 16 : START to be aware of your child's desire for free play, instruction, and team play, each in varying amounts. The integration of these options contributes to your child's individuality and prepares him or her for life and its many choices.

Help Your Child Get FIT
(Free Play, Instruction, and Team Play)

As your child becomes more coordinated and interested in group activities, play groups and school, the prospects of classes, lessons, and team sports all come into play. Your child's choices seem infinite, and the participation costs can become staggering. What activities, music, dance, art, or sports should your child embrace? How structured should your child's programs be? At what age should your child begin to increase his or her participation?

Your goal as a parent is to help your child become aware of activities that are available, depending on his or her age. Give your child options to choose from. Let your child try as many activities during free play as possible. If a particular activity seems to engage interest and he or she wants to pursue it, find out where further instruction or the opportunity to participate on a higher level is available. Keep in mind that classes and lessons can be demanding. They require time and determination on your child's part, as well as your patience and financial support.

The Real Fitness

It is very important that your child participates in active play and begins to understand the meaning of "being fit." A survey by the President's Council on Physical Fitness and Sports shows that American children have become fatter since the 1960s. This may be related to the fact that youth fitness in the United States has not improved in the last ten years, and in some cases has declined.[13]

Sports provide an excellent means for girls and boys to achieve proper levels of physical fitness. Team sports can develop a number of positive characteristics if the right philosophy exists in the program. Along with providing exercise, a good sports program also teaches children the value of cooperation, fair play, teamwork, good sportsmanship, doing your best, and learning new skills.

Sports are important both in a child's life and in an adult's. When a child participates in a sport, two attitudes should prevail. One is for the child: "Let me win. But if I cannot win, let me be brave in the attempt." (This is the Special Olympics Oath.) The second attitude is for the parent: "Child first, sport second" (a motto used for coaches and parents at the Lakewood-Trumbull YMCA in Monroe, CT).

As director of one of the largest youth basketball programs in our area (over 600 participants), it was my job to project this positive philosophy to the staff and volunteers. Those who volunteered to be part of the program believed in this doctrine and extended it through their actions. It meant the proper teaching of athletic skills, the development of team spirit and cooperation, and the building of each child's confidence through participation and positive feedback. This philosophy was instilled at the kindergarten level where children were given constant reinforcement. We made certain accommodations, such as lowering baskets so children with lesser skill levels would have greater success. This positive attitude was carried to competitive high school leagues where fair play and good sportsmanship were the major focus.

In line with the "child first, sport second" philosophy, I'd like to share with you some valuable guidelines formulated by sportscaster Jim Simpson regarding children and sports:

•Make sure that your child knows that—win or lose, scared or heroic—you love him/her, appreciate his/her efforts, and are not disappointed in him/her.

•Try your best to be completely honest about your child's athletic capability, competitive attitude, sportsmanship, and actual skill level.

•Be helpful . . . but don't coach your child on the way to the rink, track, or court . . . or on the way back . . . or at breakfast.

•Teach your child to enjoy the thrill of competition. Don't say, "Winning doesn't count," because it does.

•Try not to relive your athletic life through your child in a way that creates pressure. Don't pressure him or her because of your pride.

•Don't compete with the coach. Remember, in many cases, the coach is a hero to his or her athletes, a person who can do no wrong.

•Don't compare the skill, courage, or attitudes of your child with that of other members of the squad or team.

•Get to know the coach so that you can be happy exposing your child to his or her philosophy, attitude, ethics, and knowledge.

•Always remember that children tend to exaggerate, both when praised and when criticized. Temper your reactions when your child brings home tales of woe or heroics.

•Make a point of understanding courage and the fact that it is a relative trait. Some of us climb mountains, but we fear a fight; some of us fight, but we turn to jelly if a bee buzzes nearby. Your child must know that courage is not the absence of fear, but, rather, doing something in spite of fear.[14]

Playgrounds

Suburban towns and schools are beginning to realize the importance of play. Within the past few years more schools have begun researching and hiring consultants to design, with children's input, playgrounds where children will play for more than ten minutes. Two such "purposeful" playgrounds are near our home, and children use them constantly. Although the consultants were paid, all the materials and labor were donated to these excellent community projects. The end results are interesting, safe, durable, large playgrounds that stimulate children *and* adults. The playgrounds are combinations of climbing structures, slides, swings, bridges, rings, balancing beams, ladders, and tires. One playground also has picnic tables, a sandbox area, and a gazebo.

Exciting playground arrangements provide a multitude of benefits for children. The setup promotes plenty of exercise in climbing, swinging, jumping, sliding, and crawling. The shape of the playground will vary, but it provides endless climbing routes. In addition, the playground invites children to be creative and view the setup as a variety of different play environments. They may turn playground equipment into a castle, boat, airplane, truck, house, or a tunnel. I've seen children bring props and dress up to enhance this imaginative play. At one playground structure a boy brought his sword and eye patch and was having a great time pretending to be a pirate. This caught the attention of my son, who asked what the patch was for. It became Dad's turn to become creative as I explained what a pirate was.

The best feature of any playground is that it makes the parent an active participant in play. The majority of parents end up sliding, squeezing through, and scaling the playground structures to keep up with their children. For younger children, playgrounds give their parents time "to be there if needed." They can also praise Johnny or Judy on how well he or she is climbing. In either case, playground time is a "win-win" situation. Playgrounds, playthings, and playtime are essential for children, and they can become essential for their parents, too.

"In bringing up children, spend on them half as much money and twice as much time."

—Dr. Laurence J. Peter

5

Creating a Lifetime of Memories

"Childhood is like the old joke about a small town: one blink and it's gone. Appreciate every moment—don't wish your children's childhood away."

—*Randi Leifer*

My wife, Sue, clearly recalls one night when she went camping with her parents, three sisters, and one brother. This particular night seemed to be a normal night of camping. Everyone was asleep by 10:00. Sue's mother, Erma, woke at about 3:00 A.M. and did what most parents would do— she checked on all her sleeping children . . . one, two, three, four . . . four. . . . Where's the fifth? Her youngest daughter, Wendy (2), was not in her cot!

Erma frantically woke up her husband. The tent was very small, so where could Wendy have gone? After waking the other children, they started to search outside. The campground was filled with screams of "Wendy, where are you?" After what seemed like hours, Sue's family returned to their tent, frightened and worried. That is when they saw Wendy climbing out from under her cot! During the night she had slipped off the cot and was hidden from sight. Despair turned to great relief, but Erma did not leave Wendy's side for the rest of the trip.

What began as an ordinary camping trip, a time to relax and appreciate the outdoors, turned into a family memory that would be remembered for a lifetime. Camping has a tendency to initiate a bountiful supply of memories that a family can share over and over again.

Reminiscing with relatives and friends is a typical activity at parties or reunions. It rekindles heartfelt relationships for everyone. You can never hear those special stories too many times, and with each telling you can relive some of the circumstances and feelings that took place long before. Shared memories are part of a family's folklore, and they provide a lasting link from one generation to the next. Even serious/sad events of the past create a lasting connection between family members and those who hear the stories in years to come, although time has a way of turning many of these one-time horror stories into more humorous recollections.

Now consider that your child's everyday experiences also are stored as memories. It's obvious that you have to be actively involved with your child today to hold a place in his or her memories tomorrow.

START IS: SHAPING TOMORROW'S ADULTS BY REACHING OUT TODAY

DAY 17 : START planning and carrying out spontaneous activities with your child. These everyday episodes will turn into special lifetime memories.

Remember the Time When . . .

Memories—we all have them. Some memories are recollections of things that happened just yesterday. We remember certain times and activities more easily than others. These are the experiences that provide us with vivid lifelong memories, events I call the "unforgettables." We associate these times with specific emotions and specific visual images. Some of these memories may live as family stories, told over and over again; "unforgettable" memories usually remain vivid even after many years have passed. Some of these memories will be positive, others negative; some may be centered on major events, while many have to do with everyday occurrences. Whatever the experience, it can most likely be classified into one of four memory categories. These four groupings will act as a catalyst to help you remember your special childhood memories and to help you initiate memorable times for you and your child:

1. *Emotional times* come from experiences that have had a strong emotional impact, such as feeling sadness at the loss of a pet, being afraid of diving off the board at summer camp, worrying about the illness of a close relative, having a furious fistfight with a classmate, or the humiliation of forgetting your lines in the school play.

2. *Special times* are occasions that are particularly meaningful and significant to a child (or an adult), like learning to read, riding a bike to the store alone, getting a new puppy, going to summer camp, or traveling to another country.

3. *Great times* are the fun, thrilling, and happy times—experiences that are truly enjoyable and without incident.

4. *Crazy times* are unique experiences that involve "you had to be there" encounters.

Let's see how each one of these might look from your child's perspective.

An Emotional Time

As the program director administering our local YMCA parent/child activities, I set up a "Trail Blazer" program for fathers and their fourth-through sixth-grade sons. This age group needs active and exciting activities, and so do their fathers. We chose a white-water canoe trip down the Housatonic River in Connecticut as one of our monthly activities.

The fathers and sons were given proper instruction on safety and paddling techniques along with advice on how to go down the river. They were told that the hardest part would be at the West Cornwall covered bridge. If anyone was unsure of managing this part of the trip, they could bypass the rapids and carry their canoe on a trail along the side of the river.

The group was ready, and we set off down the Housatonic. The beginning portion of the river was very enjoyable. As we neared the covered bridge, I motioned for everyone to paddle to the side of the river. At this point we would decide who was going to continue on the river and who would be taking the land route. One by one, the father and son teams decided they wanted to "shoot the rapids." As might be expected with many boys this age, no one wanted to concede to walking at this point.

As the first canoes went through the rapids, everyone looked like they were doing fine. But as Sue and I passed under the bridge, we saw one canoe with a father and two sons get struck by a wave, catapulting the two boys in different directions. The father's face became terror-stricken. As he clutched the canoe, he saw his two sons floating down the river. Quickly, two other father and son teams paddled to retrieve the boys. The father let go of his canoe and swam toward shore, joining the rest of the group. The father and his two sons, although shaken up and wet, were fine.

There is no doubt that these three will remember this life-threatening experience for a lifetime. In fact, it will probably become part of their family's oral tradition and be passed down to grandchildren one day. These kinds of dramatic experiences tend to be few and far between. For a child, simple everyday activities comprise many more of the memories that are meaningful, memories that really "count."

A Special Time

Janet Martin, in *Daily Guideposts 1981*, recounts the story of a very successful businessman who found time one Saturday to take his twelve-year-old son fishing. An achiever, this man considered leisure an extravagance.

After a long day spent catching nothing, the pair returned home. "Waste of time," the man grumbled to his wife that night as they got ready for bed. "Didn't accomplish a thing."

"Maybe this will change your mind," his wife said, handing him a small book. "Danny showed it to me when I was helping him with his homework."

It was the youngster's diary, and the entry read simply: "Best day of my life. Dad and I went fishing."

It changed more than the man's mind. It changed the man.[1]

A simple activity? Yes! A special day? For the child, it was the "best day of my life."

"What a Great Time!"

Every day there are opportunities for enjoying time with your child, and this time need not be planned. Sometimes great moments together just happen, and often you may not realize how significant the time was until days, months, or even years later.

I remember one typical New England winter—by February it was becoming too long. I decided one afternoon, before "cabin fever" took over, to take Ryan outside. After bundling up my son with four or five layers of clothes, we ventured outdoors. Our goal was simply to get some fresh air and enjoy the outdoors.

We walked around the backyard and headed towards the woods. I noticed that the icy stream was beginning to thaw. We walked closer to the stream and I tossed a snowball into the water. Ryan, like any other two-year-old, quickly did the same. We tossed many snowballs into the stream, trying to hit objects, trying to make shapes in the water, and just throwing snowballs for the sake of throwing them. Ryan did not want to stop. I complied, and why not? We had nothing else to do at the time. Finally, Ryan reached the limit of his attention span and we headed inside. I had enjoyed the time with him, but I did not think too much about it until nearly four months later. One day Ryan and I were mowing the lawn near the stream, and I saw his face gleam with a very happy smile—he was remembering throwing snowballs in the stream! A seemingly uneventful day became a significant memory for him. What a great time that was—for both of us!

"You Had to Be There!"

As simple as it may sound, when you spend time together as a family, "good times" even "crazy times," just happen.

It was an ordinary Monday evening, or so we thought, as we invited our neighbors over with their two children for dessert. While the adults were in the living room discussing work and the children's school concerns, the children were playing quietly down in the family room. When dessert time was announced, the children and adults gathered to enjoy chocolate cake and ice cream. The conversation centered on how Lucille (the mother of the two children) had won a radio contest that morning by imitating Joan Rivers. We immediately requested a reenactment of that morning's show. This was followed by some singing of a favorite song that came on the radio while we were talking.

At this point, I sensed that a crazy performance was about to be unveiled. I quickly searched out two microphones and a blank cassette tape. After a short time convincing everyone to participate in a sing-along, we put on some favorite records and recorded our accompaniment to the songs. This was followed by jokes, riddles, funny stories, and more sing-a-longs. *Hilarious* does not adequately describe the two hours of amusement this merriment provided. We saved the tape and replay it often to relive that night.

I didn't realize the significance of that evening until I overheard our neighbor's two children recounting the jubilant events with Cindy, a twelve-year-old girl who lives in our neighborhood. She responded with a disappointed, "Boy, our family never does anything like that!" Craziness, sure, but it's healthy fun for all involved, and it came out of spending a "quiet" evening with our neighbors.

Tradition

It's been a yearly event for over eight years. It stirs up more excitement than any of the holidays. Our family and friends start thinking about it right after the Fourth of July, and we talk about it nonstop until that special weekend in October. It has become a tradition.

Each year, our group reserves a cabin in the Berkshires of Massachusetts for "a weekend away from it all." What started as a weekend for eight adults has become a weekend for a group of thirty, including twelve children. Although the place is the same each year, it provides new and exciting memories for everyone involved, like unexpected snowstorms, volleyball in the rain, midnight walks in the fog, lost adults, and a pumpkin-carving contest.

Some things stay the same—Saturday night dinner is always spaghetti—and some things are different—table tennis one year, canoe races the next. The weather tends to provide an obstacle on at least one of the three days, and usually one person does not enjoy the full weekend due to illness. There are also assorted accidents, minor disagreements, and hiking misadventures.

One such mishap remains very vivid in my mind and also in the memory of a nine-year-old child.

I thought it was a good idea. Our neighbors would be attending this getaway fall weekend as they did the previous year. Our neighbor's children, Matthew (9) and his sister Andrea (6) were excited about the many activities that would take place. Matthew and I talked about the possibility of boating and fishing, if the weather permitted. He told me he did not have a fishing pole, at which point I gave him mine to bring along. He seemed grateful and excited.

Friday night, when most everyone was arriving, was busy at the cabin. The large family room became a gathering place for family greetings and reunions. The busy, joyous conversations were cut short when Matthew's father violently motioned for me to come to his room. I found Matthew on the floor, tightly clutching his hand, which had a fish hook embedded in it. I felt dreadful and somewhat responsible for this accident, given that it was my fishing pole at the end of the hook and line.

After an intense struggle to provide the emergency relief Matthew needed, we got the hook out with very little damage to the palm of his hand. Once the commotion settled, I took the opportunity to interview Matthew on video tape in an attempt to relieve any remaining tension. Fortunately, Matthew thoroughly enjoyed the rest of the weekend. When he went back to school on Monday, this traumatic situation somehow took on the appearance of a very heroic episode. A few years have passed since the experience, but when those special weekends are discussed, Matthew and I easily begin reminiscing about the night "he caught himself fishing."

What's the bottom line when it comes to memories? *You have to be with a child today to be in his or her memories tomorrow.* Even if the experience doesn't turn out the way you had planned it, the time will still be special because you experienced something together. Think about the activities you can share with your child to build a base of strong memories, which in turn will build a closer relationship.

DAY 18 : START to create the Three R's—routines, rituals, and the ridiculous in your child's life. These are the seeds that transform everyday events into childhood "unforgettables."

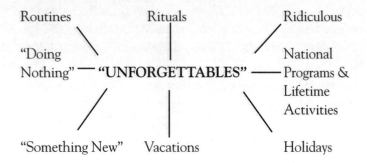

The Three "R's" of Memory-Making

It's easy to tell when a child is enjoying an activity. Kids smile, shout with joy, laugh out loud, and become intensely involved when they are having fun. Younger children find excitement in familiar activities, and they enjoy repetition. They love the Three R's of rituals, routines, and the ridiculous.

Rituals are special observances, ceremonies or celebrations, and they are very important to children. They are regular events that can be formal or informal, but regardless of formality they provide emotional security and reinforce family bonds. Rituals are usually executed in a similar manner each time they are observed. In a child's world, and on a child's level of understanding, there is always a certain procedure and order of events that must be followed. As long as parents understand this, everyone is happy. And the entire family can look forward to this special time.

Whenever Sue or I come home, or whenever we pick Ryan up at his grandparents' house, we experience a gratifying ritual with our son. Essentially our ritual is a round of "hide-'n-seek." If Ryan knows that one of us is coming home, it's instant pandemonium until he finds a good hiding spot. Then we must search for him, looking in various places before we find him. His delight in welcoming us home in this way is utterly contagious. I'm not quite sure when this ritual started, but it has become exciting for all three of us and it's a great way to "leave the work day behind."

Routines are pleasurable activities without the abundant enthusiasm and zeal of rituals. Examples include cooking a favorite meal, visiting the usual park or playground, or reading in a certain chair. Routines instill security and consistency, essential feelings for children. In our family, bedtime involves a nightly routine. After Ryan and Zachary take baths and brush their teeth, I bring Ryan into his room and he selects one or two books. After I tuck him into bed, Mom usually has the honor of reading the books to him. We recap the day's events and give bedtime hugs and kisses. The routine is completed by a song or two sung by Mom, with the lights off. This routine gave Ryan peaceful satisfaction and subsequently made his "quiet time" relaxing and content.

And then there's the *ridiculous*, those everyday activities with a twist—performing a normal activity with a new prop or act. Some "ridiculous" activities in our household involved having a tug-a-war with pieces of popcorn, serving one cookie on a large tray, singing "Old MacDonald" and replacing the animals in the song with other objects, or saying good night with a hat on or a plastic shovel in my hand. It's ridiculous, but it's lots of fun for the family.

Each of the Three R's has an aspect that a child looks forward to. A ritual is special. A routine has consistency. And the ridiculous has spontaneity. Be aware of these opportunities. Take advantage of them. Above all, enjoy them!

Assistance, Not Replacement

There are many organizations and agencies that can provide growth opportunities for you and your child. The seven major organizations listed here can help broaden your child's interests, shape his or her values, and promote lifelong parent participation in activities. They provide services nationwide that give a child the opportunity to participate in many of the activities from the Six Activity Groups—arts and crafts, dance and drama, hobbies, music, outdoor activities, and sports and games (see Chapter 4 for details on each). These organizations are:

- Boys Clubs of America
- Boy Scouts of America
- Girls Clubs of America
- Girl Scouts of America

- National 4-H Program
- YMCA or YMHA
- YWCA or YWHA

Participation in one of these organizations often sets the scene for very special times between a parent and a child.

Christine (6) had just started Brownies. Although she was a bit apprehensive about participating, she quickly discovered that carrying the flag was part of the opening ceremony. Each week she looked forward to the possibility of carrying the flag. Whenever she had the honor, she proudly and enthusiastically marched into the family room carrying the flag to announce the opening of the Brownies' troop meeting.

Although it was a simple task, carrying the flag was important, meaningful, and enjoyable for Christine. In future years, as Christine looks back, her memories of that first year in the Brownies will center on her "important role."

The type of experience you and your child have in any of these national groups will depend on two factors:

- The organization and commitment of your local chapter. Although there are national guidelines for each program, it is the local chapter, its administration, and volunteers that are the major determinants of success in your community.

- Your level of involvement and participation as a volunteer and parent. It is easy to allow other interested parents or volunteers to fill the role you should play with your child in a program. Remember that while organizations are excellent contributors to a child's growth, they do not try to replace the important role of a parent.

DAY 19 : START helping your child build a good foundation for a lifetime of meaningful, fun activities. This will expand your child's "free time" options and generate interests you can both share.

Stepping-Stones to Lifetime Activities

Whether or not you choose to join a national organization or participate in its programs, you should begin to focus on activities that you and your child can share for a lifetime. Optimally, you and your child can participate in these "lifetime activities" now and continue to share them for many years to come.

Outdoor or sports-related lifetime activities include bicycling, bowling, camping, fishing, golf, hiking, skating (ice, roller, or in-line), skiing, and tennis. Generally speaking, these are individual activities that allow regular participation by a few people. They are ideal when a team is not available for games such as softball or football, or when special equipment and facilities are not available for activities such as gymnastics and horseback riding. These activities are popular with both children and adults.

The earlier you expose your child to any indoor or outdoor activity, the more likely it is that he or she will develop it as a lifetime interest. As your child matures, there will be additional opportunities for you to share activities. Soon you will both develop similar interests that will provide a lifetime of enjoyment. What's important is that you start participating with your child in some activities today. Before you choose a specific activity, consider the following:

•Safety is a major factor in any activity.

•Be aware of your child's developmental age and gauge his or her readiness and attention span.

•Make sure the activity stays enjoyable for your child.

•The level of your child's interest will somewhat reflect your enthusiasm and the amount of time you spend together doing the activity.

The following ten activities may be introduced to your child at a very young age, as long as you adapt them to suit your child's age and developmental levels. Following the description of each activity is a listing of what I call "turn-off factors" and "creative solutions" to the turn-offs. These will help you focus on the downside of each activity from your child's point of view. Do your best to accommodate your child. For example, if you are introducing your child to biking, don't plan a ten-mile trip the first time out! Also, stop an activity *before* your child loses interest. If you stop while your child is still having fun, he or she will be delighted to come back to this activity again. That, after all, is your goal.

• *Bicycling* is an activity you can start as soon as your child reaches his or her first birthday. Before my two sons could walk, I took my them to the playground and to the store in a child carrier on my ten-speed bicycle. Bicycling can start with Big Wheels and plastic ride-on cars, followed by tricycles and two-wheelers with training wheels. By the time kids get their first real bicycle, they will be fully familiar with biking as a sport.

"Turn-off factors" may include the length of a bike ride or an uncomfortable seat, or young children may feel uneasy about riding on the road with cars. If these factors become stumbling blocks, it might be an opportune time to have a bicycle rodeo—a challenging, but safe, obstacle course set up in a driveway or empty parking lot. Set up cones, ramps, and other obstacles to maneuver around for a fun-filled riding experience.

• Children's *bowling* sets are available in wood and plastic. They can be used indoors and outdoors. Getting a child involved in "real" bowling will have to wait unless you have duckpin (small balls) bowling lanes in your area or find a bowling center that has foam pads that can be put down in the gutters. The Youth Bowling Alliance organizes leagues called Pee Wee Bowling for children ages three to seven.

"Turn-off factors" might be rolling gutter balls or getting a low score and using heavy bowling balls. But you and your child don't even need to go to a bowling alley for bowling fun. By using rubber balls and smaller pins made of plastic bottles you simulate bowling in a confined area at home. In this way children of all ages can participate.

•It's never too early to introduce your child to *camping* and the pleasures of the outdoors. Camping can be as rugged as backpacking with sleeping bags and tents or as easy as staying overnight in a recreational vehicle. Camping is one of the activities families remember most.

"Turn-off factors" might take the form of bugs, unfamiliar (scary) places, or bad weather. Setting up a tent in the backyard provides a great deal of pleasure and offers the refuge of your house if bugs are too pesky or the weather is uncooperative.

•*Fishing* is a great sport for kids. There's the thrill of the "hunt," the wonder of actually being able to feed yourself from nature, the suspense of waiting for a fish to bite, and the satisfaction of learning how to hook a worm, cast a line, reel it in and, hopefully, take a fish off the hook. Even though I grew up near a popular fishing creek, I didn't start fishing until I was sixteen! Since then I've realized that even when you don't catch anything, fishing has a special way of being enjoyable. It allows you to escape life's daily concerns and can almost "make time stand still" for you and your child.

The major "turn-off factors" can be yucky bait, the long length of time without "a catch", and sunburn while fishing in a boat. For younger children, fishing should not involve a real fishing pole (for safety reasons), but there are other fun fishing activities to do. Children can use a pole with a magnet as the "hook" to fish indoors for plastic eggs with magnets in them. We used to call this "Easter egg fishing." Or use the pole to catch some fish in a "cardboard lake" stocked with two-inch fishes made of small pieces of cardboard with a staple in it. (This game is still available in certain toy stores such as the Early Learning Centers.)

•The backyard is a great place to begin "whacking the *golf ball*." Start with plastic clubs for the tots, junior size clubs with plastic balls for older children, and then progress to a golfing range and then onto the course. Miniature golf is guaranteed fun for any age, at any time.

"Turn-off factors" for golf include the real skill needed to play the game consistently well and the patience to develop it, and the time-consuming task of completing even nine holes of golf (due to the popularity of the game, many courses are crowded). For a spontaneous game of golf, dig a few holes in your yard, bury some soup cans, and tee off for a round of homemade miniature golf.

•To initiate an interest in *hiking*, start by taking your child for strolls in the neighborhood, then to the park, then as far as your wanderlust dictates. While hiking in the Adirondacks, I came across two fathers with their children. A girl not quite five years old ascended Phelps peak, which at an elevation of 4,161 feet is a very demanding climb. The best part was that she was enjoying it. My friend and I smiled as we reached the top and found the two fathers drinking water from their canteens and the four girls thoroughly enjoying the lollipops they had carried up.

"Turn-off factors" are that hiking can be very tiring, and bad weather can ruin a pleasant day. For those who wish to stay near home but would like an added challenge, orienteering may be a good choice. Orienteering is hiking with a map and compass toward a predetermined goal. Or join up with another parent-child team and set up orienteering courses for each other. This can be done for any amount of time on any type of terrain.

•You can *ice skate* in an indoor rink, on a "backyard rink," and on a frozen pond or lake. Double-runner skates can be used for the beginner, graduating to common figure or hockey skates.

"Turn-off factors" are frequent falling and cold weather. Besides skates, another essential for ice skating is a thermos full of hot chocolate or even a small camping stove to make a fresh cup right at the lake. And if your child's ankles become tired from the skates, a game of broomball (using brooms and a ball) while wearing sneakers or boots makes a delightful game of "hockey."

•*Roller skating* or in-line skating is an easier alternate to ice skating, since you can begin in a driveway and progress to a roller rink or track in a short period of time.

A common "turn-off factor" here is falling, with the possibility of minor scrapes and bruises. A number of toy companies have added extra features for those beginners who have difficulty controlling their skates. Fisher Price, for instance, has devised an adjustable skate that allows the beginner to choose among a "walking" setting, a "forward only" setting, and a "forward-reverse" setting.

•For *downhill skiing*, you must have an appropriate skiing facility nearby. Lessons are always available, and many ski areas offer a free day of instruction and skiing once or twice each ski season. Call the skiing center for details. As an alternative to downhill skiing, cross-country skiing offers an excellent opportunity to participate in a low-cost, easily available winter sport (you can ski in snow-covered parks, golf courses, or frozen lakes).

"Turn-off factors" may include the amount of travel time to the ski area, falling on the slopes, cold weather, and the expense of equipment and lessons. One of the appealing aspects of downhill skiing is that it is a good way for a family to get away together for an entire weekend. This allows considerable time for skiing, and it brings the family together for many other activities associated with a mini-vacation.

•One of the best lifetime sports is *tennis*. Town courts are usually available, the cost of equipment is minimal, and the amount of time involved is flexible—as brief as ten minutes or as long as a tennis weekend.

I've had the privilege of instructing tennis to many young children, and today I still see these children, now high school-age teens, playing tennis with their parents. Not only is it good exercise, but tennis is social (in the best sense of the word). Tennis is one of those shared interests that will last a lifetime for you and your child.

There is a big "turn-off factor." Tennis requires a certain amount of skill and the patience to develop this skill. Tennis is just one of many racquet games, however. Other games include badminton, racquetball, platform tennis, and paddleball, which are easier to learn in a short period of time.

Other lifetime activities may include handball, hunting, jogging, swimming, and weightlifting.

Whatever activity you chose, be sure to involve your child more than just a few times. The long-term benefits of activities are truly immeasurable. Enjoy the game. Enjoy the outdoors. Enjoy the time together.

Obviously, there are many times you will want to participate in an indoor activity with your child. Indoor activities provide you and your child the chance to share in a common, cooperative goal, such as completing a jigsaw puzzle, or to compete for fun, such as playing Monopoly. Here are just ten of the many activities that you can begin to spend some quantity time on together:

- Computer and video games
- Crossword puzzles
- Painting or drawing
- Photography
- Dancing and singing
- Cooking
- Board games such as chess, checkers, and backgammon
- Card playing
- Indoor gardening
- Table tennis and billiards

START IS: SHAPING TOMORROW'S ADULTS BY REACHING OUT TODAY

DAY 20 : START celebrating holidays and vacations in both "traditional" ways and in your own distinct family manner. The new events and customs you develop will become enjoyable family traditions.

New Holidays That Are Not on the Hallmark Calendar

Halloween is always an eventful and fun-filled holiday for our family. This year preparations started early in October. We carefully planned our costumes, decorated the house, picked and carved our pumpkins, and got "Mr. Scarecrow" ready to sit on his bench on the front lawn.

Costumes became the top priority. Since costume choices for two-month-old babies are limited, we were delighted when a friend gave us a skeleton costume for Zachary—it even glowed in the dark. Ryan and I were to have even more creative costumes—the two of us would be a pair of dice. To produce these homemade costumes, we had to select the right size boxes, make arm and head holes, paint the boxes with a thick coat of white paint, and make dots from black construction paper. These exquisite costumes met up with a rainy Halloween night, but nothing hit us that a large beach umbrella couldn't handle. The climax of Halloween evening was a visit to the "witch down the street," a woman everyone knew dressed especially for the occasion. When Ryan saw her, his earlier confidence about meeting her quickly dissolved. His frightful retreat brought us home with the resolution that next year would be a better time to meet her.

Holidays are so much fun, but gaiety and joy need not be limited to Valentine's Day, Easter, Thanksgiving, Fourth of July, Cinco de Mayo, Hanukkah, Kwanzaa, Christmas, and other major holidays. Why not create some new holidays to celebrate all year round? One great source for new celebrations and special occasions is *Chase's Annual Events*, a book you can find in any library. But to get you started, here are some ideas for three new "holidays" each month:

JANUARY

•Proclaim Hat Day on the first Saturday in January. Begin the year by keeping warm or not getting sunburned, depending on where your family lives. Gather all the hats in your household and try to wear each one sometime during the day. To complement this gala affair, add costumes, make new hats, take pictures, or exchange a hat with a friend.

•Don't forget National Nothing Day, which you can observe whenever you like. It's hard to do absolutely nothing, especially with children, so maybe you can go visit a friend or tour a museum together. Whatever you do, make sure it's a restful and peaceful time.

•January 27 (1756) is Wolfgang Amadeus Mozart's birthday. Observe this day by attending a concert, play, opera, or symphony.

FEBRUARY

• The third day of February is great for celebrating the life of Johan Gutenberg, who invented movable type in Germany in 1468 and created the first printed book. Celebrate by making a family seal or individual emblems for family members with woodcut designs or potato prints; make your own stationary.[2] Visit a library or a bookstore, too!

• The U.S. Weather Bureau was established on February 9, 1891. Make February 9 a day to enjoy the weather outdoors or, if your family is up for a craft project challenge, you can create your own home weather station.

• Commemorate Susan B. Anthony's birthday on February 15 by starting a coin collection. Open all your piggy banks to look for silver coins, "wheat" pennies, or a selection of coins for the year you were born.

MARCH

• The nation's first national park was established at Yellowstone on March 1, 1872. Celebrate with a visit to a local park.

• In the Northern Hemisphere, the first day of spring (the vernal equinox) occurs on or around March 21, depending on leap years. It is a time of newness, hope, and life. Celebrate with a New Year's Party; dig out all the party hats and noisemakers from January.

• Lyman Lipman patented the pencil with an attached eraser on March 30, 1812. Declare March 30 to be Inventors' Day at your house—gather "odds and ends" together and create a unique workable contraption.

APRIL

• The first moving-picture theater opened in Los Angeles on April 2, 1902, with an admission price of ten cents. Take the family to a movie or, even better, film or videotape some "home" movies.

• Observe National Procrastination Week (which was in March) a month late. Put off chores for a day and go to a playground or mall. Put off going to bed for an extra hour for the whole family!

•Gideon Sundback invented the zipper on April 29, 1913. Celebrate by putting on a fashion show of clothes with zippers for your family and friends.

MAY

•Pick a May day to take on the "Visit-A-Park Challenge." Visit as many parks in your town as you can during one afternoon. Make a nature craft at each park.

•Charles Lindburgh flew across the Atlantic on May 21, 1927. Visit the nearest airport and have lunch there; if possible, take the family for a short airplane or helicopter flight.

•May is an excellent month for gardening . . . and digging for treasures. Put together a surprise package and hide it or bury it. Go treasure hunting with your child.

JUNE

•June is a popular month for the circus. Attend a circus if it's in town. If not, make up your own circus act. Take a family bike ride, visit a zoo, or enjoy an afternoon at a playground with swings and monkey bars. Rent a tank of helium and fill up lots of balloons!

•Abner Doubleday invented baseball on June 12, 1839. Take the family to a game or, better yet, organize a baseball game in your neighborhood.

•In the Northern Hemisphere, the first day of summer (the summer solstice) occurs on or around June 22. This event inaugurates the coming months of relaxation and vacations. Enjoy a day planning your summer vacation and day trips. Visit a travel agent or chamber of commerce for ideas and bring home some brochures.

JULY

•Honor Frog Month. Visit a pond or swamp and search for some frogs; catch them. Have a frog-jumping contest. Return the frogs back to their natural habitat.

• On July 20, 1969, Neil Armstrong and Edwin Aldrin landed on the moon. At 10:56 P.M., Neil Armstrong took humankind's first step on the moon. Celebrate by visiting a planetarium, or have an evening Moon Festival with a telescope. Gather your family astronomers outdoors and enjoy the moon, stars, and planets.

• The ice cream cone was invented at the St. Louis World's Fair on July 24, 1904. Bring the family together for an ice cream sundae or cone party; make some homemade ice cream.

AUGUST

• Celebrate "Let's Eat Everything That's Green" Day. Enjoy summer's fresh fruits and vegetables. If it's not green and you want to eat it, make it green with food coloring. Top off the meal with green cookies and green punch served on a green table cloth.

• Observe National Camping Day with your family. Set up camp in your backyard or porch; enjoy the final days of summer by camping outdoors for one night.

• Celebrate your pet's birthday this month, whether you have a fish, a cat, a dog, or a hamster. If you do not have a pet, visit a friend who does and celebrate with her or him.

SEPTEMBER

• Honor the Wonderful World of Trains this month. Get on the right track by visiting a toy train shop, tour a train station, or take a ride into or out of the city in a train.

• Organize your own family Kite Flying Day. On the first windy day of the season, get out your kites. If you don't have any, make your own to fly on the next windy day.

• In the Northern Hemisphere, the first day of fall (the autumnal equinox) occurs on or around September 22. Search for a grocery store or fruit stand that has begun selling pumpkins. Bring the pumpkins home and paint faces on them. Buy a bag of apples and bake an apple pie.

OCTOBER

•Henry Ford introduced the Model T on October 1, 1903. Celebrate this day by washing the car with your child and going for a family drive.

•The Great Chicago Fire took place on October 8, 1871. Make this day a fire safety day. Visit a firehouse for safety tips, and check your home for fire hazards.

•Celebrate Columbus Day, October 12, by taking a family boat ride on a lake or river, or get the family together to build a model of a ship.

NOVEMBER

•Proclaim International Pancake Day on the first Saturday or Sunday in November. Celebrate by cooking pancakes together; invite your neighbors over for pancake sampling.

•Surprise your neighbors again. Organize a championship checker, chess, or backgammon tournament. Give out gag certificates or prizes.

•Take the November Chocolate Challenge. Buy some chocolate and candy molds and make homemade chocolates. See which family member can resist indulging in the chocolate delights the longest. It can be most enjoyable being the loser in this contest!

DECEMBER

•Celebrate summer fun in December. Have a mini beach party and barbecue indoors. Bring out the blankets, portable radio, and inflatable tubes and rafts.

•Beethoven was born on December 16, 1770. Celebrate with a live family music festival. Invite friends and relatives who play instruments to participate; create new instruments and make up your own songs.

•In the Northern Hemisphere the first day of winter (the winter solstice) occurs on or around December 22. Since this falls in the middle of "the giving season," help others by visiting a hospital or nursing home, assisting with a food drive, or providing gifts for the needy.

Both the standard holidays and your family's own unique celebrations offer a special time for activities. Mark your calendar for these days. Plan appropriate activities, songs, and crafts. Each month offers a parent and child so many opportunities to share new activities and create lasting memories.

Vacations

"This is no longer a vacation; it's a quest—it's a quest for fun. I'm gonna have fun and you're gonna have fun. We're all going to have so much fun we'll need plastic surgery to remove our smiles."

From the movie, *National Lampoon's Vacation*

How are your family vacations remembered?

More than 3,000 fifth grade students were presented a list and asked, "Which of the following was the happiest moment of this past year for you?" The choices were: "getting a good grade on a test," "meeting a new friend," "getting a new brother or sister," "taking a trip," "winning a competition," or "other." The number one answer was "taking a trip."

Trips are fun and exciting. For all family members to enjoy a vacation, you have to plan one that incorporates something that everyone will enjoy.

If your company gives you vacation time, you owe it to yourself and to your family to make sure you take it. Vacations allow you to enjoy the sights and sounds of different cities, states, and countries. Whenever you get the opportunity to travel to new locations, take advantage of it. Visit specialty theme parks, museums, historical sites, and other major tourist attractions. Before your trip, utilize the helpful resources of a travel agent, library, and chamber of commerce. Dorothy Ann Jordon and Marjorie Adoff Cohen's book, *Great Vacations with Your Kids* gives detailed information for family trips throughout the United States.

But if plans, finances, or time schedules do not permit long-distance traveling, look at the opportunities in your own neighborhood, town, or city. Get your family together and plan an extraordinary vacation. Here are a few ideas to get you started:

•Take the family sightseeing for a one- or two-day car trip within fifty miles of your home. For a change of pace, stay at a "bed and breakfast" lodging.

•Go camping at a lake, mountain, or beach. Try sleeping in a tent, a cabin, or in a recreational vehicle. Invite a group of friends to join your family's camping trip.

•See if you and your family can spend a full day on a farm or ranch. (The "relaxed vacation" portion may turn out to be going back home!)

•Select from the following list of "Different Modes of Transportation" trips:

—Take a short boat cruise on a lake or river.

—Take a ride in a hot air balloon.

—Take a guided raft or canoe trip.

—Take an airplane flight over your city. Be sure to take photographs.

—Go horseback riding or take a carriage ride.

—Ride bikes or mopeds together.

•Visit the highest point in your state. Travel to the highest point in nearby states. Then visit the lowest points.

•Visit the nearest zoo. Call ahead for any special family programs—maybe you can even help clean or feed the animals.

•Browse through local flea markets or, even better, set up a booth at one of these events.

•Find out how different products are really made. Visit factories that give tours in your area—food processors, paper manufacturers, glass-blowing studios, media facilities, toymakers and sporting good plants, etc.

•Set up an appointment with a radio station or sound studio to make your own radio broadcast (not to be aired), or ask for an opportunity to record the family singing your child's favorite songs. Make a copy of the recording so you can take it home.

• Try driving your family Nowhere! Write down arbitrary directions such as "Go to first traffic light, turn right, then left, go two miles and turn left again," then see where you end up. Stop for lunch. Set a time limit. (Be sure to bring a map so you can find your way home, if you do happen to find "Nowhere.")

• Visit all the sports stadiums in your region. Get a souvenir from each. For a change of pace, request permission to visit a facility when no teams are playing. Get a picture of your family on the playing field.

• Visit three area parks. Organize a three-meal picnic for the day, with breakfast, lunch and dinner each at a different park.

• Help your family (and neighborhood) organize an art, stamp, or coin show. Share one of these new hobbies with your child.

• Start a collection of bookmarks, pencils, balloons, bottle caps, shells, leaves, or insects. Go on a "collector's hunt" to find new treasures.

The secret to enjoying vacations is to become involved and excited about them during the planning stages—even two or three months in advance. Your vacation experience can be as diverse and outrageously fun as you want it to be. Plan events that will be remembered. Remember that during any vacation, your family should be prepared for unexpected delays, dilemmas, or disappointments. It always helps to have an abundant amount of flexibility and humor. And once the vacation is over, relive it with brochures, pictures, and videos.

Ways to Enjoy Traveling with Children

Obviously, traveling will be a large part of your vacation time with the family. Enjoy this time together. Here are some useful tips that will help you all arrive safe, sound, and in good humor.

•Make it musical—sing favorite songs, play cassette tapes, use headphones (if possible) for a quiet alternative.

•Play games—small board games, games using travel scenery (such as counting similar signs), spotting out-of-state license plates, counting cows, the game of "Animal Farm" (everyone collects animals for a farm by spotting real ones, words, or pictures of them on billboards).

•Do arts and crafts—a sticker book and stickers, crayons and paper, coloring books.

•Put on a puppet show—small toys, dolls, finger puppets.

•Read books—books about the area in which you are traveling, picture books, work books, activity books.

•Write joint family letters—to Grandma and Grandpa, other relatives, neighbors, friends.

•Talk about family travels—about the last trip that was taken, what everyone wants to see on this trip.

•Tell stories—ghost stories, "add on" stories (a complete story is told as each person adds on his or her portion).

•Complete puzzles—small lap puzzles, magnetic puzzles, postcard puzzles (make them by cutting a postcard of the previous area you visited into pieces; keep them for your child to play with or send the puzzle pieces to a friend).

•Take along surprises—wrap small gifts or old forgotten toys and have your child open a new one at regular travel intervals.

•Bring snacks—pack some of your child's favorite treats, fruit, or homemade desserts.

•Stop, stretch, and snap photos—take some silly pictures, photograph historic or scenic sights, create a new family photo tradition (such as taking pictures each time you cross a state border).

Spending a family day together, whether near your home or far away, will be more enjoyable if you've made preparations in advance. Here are some helpful hints for full-day outings:

- Buy advance tickets to an event to save money.

- Bring your own food for lunch, or at least bring snacks and beverages.

- Plan the length of your stay to suit the needs of your children.

- Strollers are a must for small children, particularly if the weather is hot or if you plan to do a lot of walking.

- Use name tags and tell your child what to do if he or she gets lost.

- If you're visiting a fair or theme park, try to get a map and schedule of events beforehand.

- Since everyone may not enjoy the same activities, have everyone select a favorite activity for the day.

- Have everyone in your family wear comfortable, weather-appropriate clothes and shoes.

- Decide before your trip what you will allow your child to buy or what you will buy, if anything (i.e., souvenirs, gifts, or candy). Once you have set limits, be consistent and make no exceptions.

Going the Extra Mile

Whenever possible, take a camera with you to capture special family moments in pictures. Children love to look through photo albums. People love to look at other people, especially themselves! It brings back memories. It inspires questions and initiates conversation.

Guidelines:

- Select a camera to suit your ability, convenience, and budget.

- Leave photo albums in accessible areas of your home for regular viewing.

- When your child is old enough, have her or him take some of the family pictures.

(Note: Video cameras or camcorders are becoming more common and popular. They are truly able to "capture the moment." Consider videotaping as an option, but think about the video camera becoming a nuisance during special moments. If a video camera is too bulky, it can easily take away from your enjoyment of an activity. In addition, when you're ready to view a video, your child ends up in front of the television. Children also like to pick out the special times from a vacation, and this is much easier to do in pictures than on tape. Weigh the pros and cons of the different equipment, and select the equipment that will best suit your family's needs. Whatever your choice of equipment, the main idea is to capture those great family moments for unforgettable memories.)

"Something New"

The Hudson Valley in New York, where my family and I live, offers a number of excellent tourist sites. One special place in particular is the CIA—the Culinary Institute of America, not the government agency. The CIA is one of the nation's finest cooking schools. Included in its offerings to the community are four specialty restaurants. A dinner at any one of these is memorable because you have the opportunity to experiences some first-rate meals. Although the majority of CIA's patrons are adults, I've seen children eating in these restaurants, usually celebrating a special occasion. I've enjoyed watching them quickly discover that some very "different" meals are served here—not your common McDonald's "happy meal"! It seems that the CIA follows Jasper Johns' rule of creativity: "Take an object. Do something to it. Do something else to it." The chefs train the students to be very creative and artistic in every aspect of meal preparation. This means a chef must not only ensure that the meal is made up of the right ingredients, but he or she must make the appearance of the food very pleasing to the eye. Why not adopt this approach in the activities that you and your children participate in?

Let go of your "normal" thinking prototype for an activity and try to think of another way to play it. Imagine how to add something to it, how to make a new rule apply, or how to set aside all the rules. Follow the approach of "taking an activity, doing something to it, and do something else to it." The amazing result is that your child will quickly further your creative thinking, and new activities will soon evolve that will provide your family with much pleasure and excitement. Your child will start to come up with his or her own ideas. As long as something different is safe, why not try it? You may find yourself quickly changing from spectator to a fully involved participant. The reward will be a memorable experience that your child will probably want to relive time and time again. Try playing soccer with diving flippers on, go with your child into a tent or fort and read a book together, fly a kite in the winter. Or you can become creative in the kitchen, as Carol Knapp describes in "Something New":

One afternoon while my four children were in school, my four-year-old neighbor, Michael, came to visit. Since he is mostly full of giggles and always full of questions, I didn't expect he'd let the day pass quietly. But I was unprepared when he fastened his lively dark eyes on me and announced, "Let's make a cake."

With a sigh, I set aside my letter-writing and began rummaging in the cupboard for baking supplies. I decided we would make an apple cake. Michael chattered happily as he helped crack eggs and measure flour. When it was time to stir in the chopped apple, he spied his bag of gumdrops on the counter.

"Let's put these in, too," he suggested.

The sensible grown-up in me muttered, "You don't put gumdrops in an apple cake." He stood there looking so pleased with himself I couldn't say no. In went the gumdrops.

"I know," I said, entering his fun, "we'll call this a Michael Surprise cake!" He giggled, and the neglected child in me giggled back. (By the way, the cake was delicious!)[3]

"Doing Nothing"

There may be times that your child is bored with the usual games or activities and you just can't think of anything new. Fret not, for this may present a perfect opportunity to do nothing—well, almost nothing. Just being together can offer you precious opportunities with your child such as roughhousing, throwing rocks in puddles or streams, going for a walk in your neighborhood or back yard, or just sitting on your front steps and watching a sunset. These "nothing times" will often find a special place in your child's memories.

An early spring thaw was a welcome sight. With very little snow left and the ground turning to mud, Ryan, Zachary and I decided a walk in the woods might be our best bet. We dilly-dallied by the stream, breaking ice off the sides of rocks. We checked out the small pond where we play ice hockey with golf clubs and a plastic ring, but the ice was no longer safe. We were both content to continue this casual patrolling of the area. We enjoyed "doing nothing" outdoors and we enjoyed each other's company.

Turning back to the house, the three of us agreed to continue our walk, so we decided to take the long route home. This meant a walk past the apple orchard and a walk on a back road for approximately one-half mile. As we headed toward the apple orchard, we saw that the ground was soft and somewhat muddy. But we had boots on and we accepted the challenge set before us (at this point, going home the short route would have been much too easy). The first portion of our orchard walk was not too bad—we used rocks as stepping stones and small logs as bridges. Then we began to notice that our feet were sinking deeper into the mud and our boots were getting heavier as we lifted them. Fortunately, we all found this very humorous, and our frequent comment was "Yuck!" As we continued on, we found ourselves helping each other out of treacherous mud holes as we tried to reach the road, still 100 yards away. Our luck in the mud did not improve, but our outlook turned from hilarious to hysterical, and our comments turned into a song about "being stuck in 100 percent yuck." Following an exhausting struggle, we finally reached the road. After we cleaned this heavy-duty yuck off our boots, we felt as if we were walking on air.

Trying to "do nothing" can easily turn into an unforgettable memory *if you let it happen.* And sometimes the experiences can be enjoyed again and again. Ryan, Zachary, and I were out in the orchard at least five more times during the spring thaw, thoroughly delighted to be trudging through the 100 percent heavy-duty yuck!

My sister, three brothers, and I looked forward to the same annual event, year after year. We knew that each year brought some surprises. The day after Thanksgiving was when our family really got serious about Christmas. The living room was rearranged to accommodate a live Christmas tree, boxes of decorations were retrieved from the basement, and my father started searching for the sheet music for the Christmas carols he would play. My father enjoying playing the piano, and we owned a second-hand upright. Each day another traditional activity came to life. My mother began baking cakes and cookies. We started opening our Advent calendars on the first day of December. Before December dinners we lit the candles in our special handmade Christmas holders. We hunted outside for another "perfect" Christmas tree. And, of course, we took time out to think about gifts to add to our wish lists, which grew longer each day.

Since we lived in the Northeast region of the U.S., good snowfalls also contributed to the holiday spirit. We went sledding, built snow forts and, naturally, had frequent snowball fights. We usually stayed out until dark playing in our winter wonderland. At dusk, which comes early in the month of December, we came in willingly because we knew that after dinner our family would sing Christmas carols. My father would play the piano and the rest of us, seven in all, made up a good-sized chorus. Singing Christmas carols was an activity that everyone in our family became enchanted with. Very rarely did anyone miss this family tradition. Not only was it fun, but it provided each of us with the reassurance and the sense of belonging that comes from being part of a caring family. Family togetherness gave me the inner strength and compassion to cope with the daily harshness the world sometimes presented. I remember those Christmases as a very happy time, and it is this feeling that I hope to pass along to my children.

"The best things you can give children, next to good habits, are good memories."

—*Sydney Harris*

"Guideposts Ministries can help you the family program you are looking for....."

Guideposts offers a free 80-page *Family Information Network Database (FIND) Toll Free Number Directory*. The FIND Directory is a listing of toll free 800 numbers for helping agencies listed on the FIND files. It has been created to aid individuals and families to obtain assistance immediately. The directory is organized into 39 major subjects with over 450 different agencies.

If you would like a free copy of the Guideposts FIND Toll Free Number Directory, please complete this card and mail it to Guideposts Associates Inc. (no postage stamp is necessary). You will also receive information on FIND and how you can obtain detailed descriptions of services available from more than 2,000 national and regional organizations.

Name _____ Date _____

Address _____

City _____ State _____ Zip _____

720-5305

CHAPTER

6

I Definitely Need Some Time for Myself

"Find out for yourself the form of rest that refreshes you best."

—*Daniel Considine*

An adult's world is a busy place. Chances are your life was pretty full of things to do before you even had children. And now you're expected to be organized at home and at work, be a well-informed citizen, and a warm and loving parent at all times. Ha!

Here's a typical day in the life of a mother I'll call Alice. She's a registered nurse who works three nights a week, third shift (midnight until 8:00 A.M.), and she recently participated in a nurse's strike. Alice is the mother of three children, a boy (10) and two girls (2 and 7). The children wanted a pet that they promised they would take care of—they now have a dog and two birds. Alice's neighborhood needed a Brownie leader, so she volunteered and now organizes a weekly meeting for twelve girls. The PTA at school needed help organizing activities for the children, so she accepted the offer and assisted in putting on a Halloween party for 200 children, with more events yet to come. Alice's family appreciates the dinners and family reunions at her house, especially around the holidays. While completing errands in town, she is soliciting business appointments for her husband, who owns a home-improvement business. And the bowling team she's joined is in fourth place. Hectic? Yes indeed! Possible? Sure is.

I Definitely Need Some Time for Myself **117**

Your schedule may be very similar. You may have a different occupation, more or fewer children, no partner, different activities, but you are probably just as busy—or busier. Is it exhausting? Does it sometimes seem unending? Yes. Do you need a break from it? Definitely! Do you feel guilty even thinking about it? You bet! When the enthusiasm, positive thinking, and energy seem to have run out, parents do need time for themselves.

START IS: SHAPING TOMORROW'S ADULTS BY REACHING OUT TODAY

DAY 21 : START becoming alert to "those days" when you need rest. Being aware of this need is the first step to recovering your balance, wellness, and happiness.

It's Called Many Things

Parenting can be hard work, frustrating and tiring, and having a "lifetime" responsibility can seem like forever. There will be days when you are totally exhausted. That feeling of exhaustion is called many things—burnout, wipeout, end of the rope, losing it, famished. Being overwhelmed by parenting can take place at any time, but it usually manifests itself as sickness, an overload of stress, a need to participate in a favorite activity, a desire to be with other adults, and particularly as a desire to be away from children.

Once you've decided that you need or want some time for yourself, it's not always easy to justify arranging a break. When you're sick, you have no choice. If your healthcare professional has recommended rest, either a day in bed or a week at home, share this information with your child. She or he will understand. Child care help from relatives and friends at this time may prove invaluable. Please realize that if you don't take care of yourself, you will be setting a poor example for your child, and you will put yourself at risk of becoming even sicker.

It's difficult to just allow ourselves to take time off or claim some private time, although most people do recognize the legitimacy of doing so when they're "stressed out."

Stress (in psychology) is a demand, threat, or other event that requires an individual to cope with a changed situation. Stressors are an unavoidable part of life. They range in severity from relatively mild forms, such as a traffic jam, a disparaging remark from an employer or a family argument, to severe ones, such as being fired or experiencing the death of a partner. People's responses to stress vary widely, depending on their cultural and family background, their personal experiences, their present mood and on other stressors present at the same time. Most people are able to cope satisfactorily with the everyday stresses of living. However, when problems escalate faster than they can be solved, a person's adaptive capacity may be overloaded and chronic illness, anxiety, or depression may result.[1]

Two American psychiatrists, Thomas H. Holmes and Richard Rahe, devised the Social Readjustment Ratings Scale, which ranks forty-three critical stressors according to the severity of their impact on an individual's life.

The Social Readjustment Rating Scale[2]

Life Event	Mean Value
1. Death of spouse	100
2. Divorce	73
3. Marital separation	65
4. Jail term	63
5. Death of close family member	63
6. Personal injury or illness	53
7. Marriage	50
8. Fired at work	47
9. Marital reconciliation	45
10. Retirement	45
11. Change in health of family member	44
12. Pregnancy	40
13. Sex difficulties	39
14. Gain of new family member	39
15. Business readjustment	39

Life Event	Mean Value
16. Change in financial state	38
17. Death of close friend	37
18. Change to different line of work	36
19. Change in number of arguments with spouse	35
20. Mortgage over $10,000	31
21. Foreclosure of mortgage or loan	30
22. Change in responsibilities at work	29
23. Son or daughter leaving home	29
24. Trouble with in-laws	29
25. Outstanding personal achievement	28
26. Wife begins or stops work	26
27. Begin or end school	26
28. Change in living conditions	25
29. Revision of personal habits	24
30. Trouble with boss	23
31. Change in work hours or conditions	20
32. Change in residence	20
33. Change in schools	20
34. Change in recreation	19
35. Change in church activities	19
36. Change in social activities	18
37. Mortgage or loan less than $10,000	17
38. Change in sleeping habits	16
39. Change in number of family get-togethers	15
40. Change in eating habits	15
41. Vacation	13
42. Christmas	12
43. Minor violations of the law	11

Stress involves change, whether it's positive or negative. The stressors on the Holmes and Rahe scale include stressful times related to parenting. The following list will alert you to potentially stressful circumstances and periods within child-rearing. Hopefully some stress for you and your family will be alleviated simply by expecting it.

First Year
Premature baby
Medical costs
New schedule for parents—day and evening
New responsibility
Feeding—bottle vs. breast
Crying
Colic
Teething
Sickness
Shots
Child care
Diapers—cloth versus disposable
Nursery setup
The circumcision issue
Sleep deprivation
"Advice" from friends and relatives
Change in relationship between husband and wife
Postpartum blues
Career vs. child-raising—or balancing the two

Second Year
Toilet training
Sickness
Child care/sitters
Temper tantrums and saying "no"
Child-proofing the house
Weaning from breast or bottle
Child's anxiety and fears (strange people, nightmares, phobias)
Feeding problems
Speech/hearing disorders

Three to Five Years
Nursery school
Manners
Room clean-up
Television
Siblings—a new baby and/or sibling rivalry
Accidents and injuries
Bed-wetting
Aggressive behavior
Separation anxiety

Six to Eight Years
Friends
School
Chores
Competition
Religion
Allowances
Television/movies
Sexual awareness/privacy

Nine to Twelve Years
Being part of a group
Rebellion
Peer influence
School
Summer vacations/camps
Injuries
Puberty
The opposite sex
Substance abuse
AIDS awareness and sex education

We Received Our Initiation Early

A newborn can be demanding as well as enchanting. Our first year with Ryan turned out to be more stressful than Sue and I had expected. Our son had intestinal problems, or colic, which affects from 9 to 23 percent of newborns. Children with colic suffer acute abdominal pains and are unable to sleep comfortably. Because of Ryan's colic, my wife and I were up regularly during many evenings trying to comfort our newborn son. For awhile we thought his crying was normal, at least until he got used to his new surroundings. After innumerable sleepless nights and much uneasiness, we took Ryan to our family physician. The recommended prescription provided little relief. Family and friends thought they were helping us by sharing "home remedies" for Ryan. Time ended up being the most effective remedy of all. After twelve months, we began to feel that life was becoming somewhat normal. We have since discovered that many other parents have had a colicky baby and can sympathize with us. Sue and I also learned that we should have taken a few breaks that first year to help alleviate the stress of that extremely difficult time.

As I look back, I realize this stressful episode produced a bond between Ryan and me that I could never have anticipated. I was forced to spend time with my child even if I was not interested or prepared to. To care for my vulnerable son, I had to become completely unmindful of myself. I had to give something that was cherished by all non-parents—my time—especially when sleep was beckoning. I discovered that the giving of a good quantity of my time was my way of loving this child, and this sacrifice yielded much in return. It developed a genuine closeness between the two of us that never may have developed otherwise. It was this commitment of my quantity time that led to a better understanding of my role as a parent. I felt a sense of fulfillment with Ryan that would continue to grow.

Each stage of your child's development will yield difficulties and hard times. As a concerned and loving parent, you will not be able to avoid or erase these challenging times, but you can be better prepared both mentally and physically. Parents should become familiar with the expected situations and circumstances that are part of each period of a child's growth. There are three ways you can be prepared and learn what to expect during stressful times of change: read up on the topics, talk them over with other parents, and consult healthcare professionals.

Options

As you look back to the "hard times," you can begin to understand and recognize how you have grown through child-rearing experiences. But what about the times when stress is overwhelming? What can you do now that will help immediately? Here are some stress-reducing options you can explore:

• *Exercise* is an excellent outlet for relieving stress, both on a short-term and long-term basis. Exercise gives you an opportunity to escape from a stressful situation, at least for a brief time. While participating in an active exercise program, you experience an immediate release of bottled-up frustration and energy. The long-range benefit is that those people who exercise live longer than those who don't, due to the temporary elimination of stress and the increased health of the body.

If you have not been physically active, be sure to get a doctor's physical examination before undertaking any exercise program. This will alert you to your present level of fitness and the limits you should impose upon yourself as you start a new exercise program. Whatever your physical condition may be, walking is an excellent and easy way to begin an exercise program. It provides short-term relief stress and long-term health.

• Find the form and amount of *rest* you need and make this a priority during stressful times. Rest provides your body with the opportunity to recover. Aside from sleep, you may want to try meditation, another form of relaxation.

• *Reach out by sharing* your concerns with family, friends, or caring professionals. Another avenue of sharing is to use your time to help others, which will allow you to focus your thoughts and energy positively—temporarily away from your own problems. Helping others will also help put your concerns into healthier perspective.

• *Be prepared* the next time you face parenting challenges. Practice some preventative medicine; give yourself permission to take time out before sickness and stress hit. Don't let the situation go that far!

Think of Yourself First for a Change

Here is a four-step thought process which you can use to help keep child-rearing stress to a minimum:

1. *Take time out.* Take a break. Give yourself a rest, both mentally and physically. Find some quiet time for yourself. Take a break from work, family, or whatever seems to be stifling you. Take a deep breath and continue on.

2. *Take a step back.* Pull yourself away from the problem. Look at the situation and its relationship to the big picture, your life. Measure its significance and the amount of energy that you should expend on it. Ask others to help you put the situation into perspective.

3. *Plan a course of action.* Make a decision to take the appropriate action, change direction, complete a process—whatever needs to be done to deal with or overcome the overwhelming situation.

4. *Take heart,* for "this too shall pass." Realize that although the particular problem you face may seem devastating, it will eventually pass. With the right attitude and proper action, you can face each and every situation. Realize that you can look back on each stressful situation as a learning experience.

START IS: SHAPING TOMORROW'S ADULTS BY REACHING OUT TODAY

DAY 22 : START contacting helping agencies and services, including support groups, when the need arises. These resources will assist you in overcoming the rough times in parenting.

Children go through many stages of growth and much transition. There will be times when you find yourself in an overwhelmingly complex predicament as a parent, wondering how to cope with your changing child. It is important to realize that you do not have to face these difficult situations alone. There are many options and services available when help is needed. The important step is to reach out—sometimes help is as close as your bookshelf; other times you'll find it at professional agencies in the community.

Information

Sometimes you will only need a "pick me up" bit of child-rearing wisdom or some information to deal with a particular parenting situation. Here are some ideas:

•*Books, magazines, and videos.* Through these materials experts provide knowledge in all areas of parenting, education, health and recreation. Make use of your local library or bookstore to find information on your particular child-rearing interests or concerns. Select helpful books in the areas of child development such as *Your Baby and Child—from Birth to Age Five* by Penelope Leach; *Infants and Mothers* or *Toddlers and Parents* by T. Berry Brazelton, M.D.; or one of three books by Theresa Caplan—*The First Twelve Months of Life, The Second Twelve Months of Life* and *The Early Childhood Years*; a child care book such as *Dr. Spock's Baby and Child Care* by Dr. Benjamin Spock and Dr. Michael B. Rothenberg, or *New Baby Book* by Better Homes and Gardens; a prescription drug guide such as *Prescription Drugs* by the editors of *Consumer Guide*; an activity or play book such as *1001 Things to Do With Your Kids* by Caryl Waller Krueger or *Toy Buying Guide* by Consumers Reports; and an inspirational book such as *Love You Forever* by Robert Munsch, *The Giving Tree* by Shel Silverstein or *Hope for the Flowers* by Trinna Paulus (which I recommend for parents and children).

Among the numerous magazines available to parents, look into *American Baby Magazine, Child, Children, Christian Parenting, Family Fun, Family Life, Parenting,* and *Parents.*

A variety of parenting videos have flooded the market. Before buying these videos, check your local library for free rentals. Also look into video stores (such as Blockbuster Videos) that may have a community service section of educational videos that are loaned free. Two videos which you should view are Nova's *The Miracle of Life* and Children's Television Workshop production *What Kids Want to Know About Sex and Growing Up.*

•*Family Resource Centers.* A Family Resource Center is a neighborhood-based center offering programs that emphasizes education for families and the prevention of serious problems within families. Family Resource Centers offer integrated family-focused services at the neighborhood level that support parents in their parenting role, promote optimal childhood development, enhance family functioning, strengthen the informal needs of families, and link families to other services not provided by the center. Check with your school, town hall, or telephone directory for a center in your area.

•*Social agencies.* All municipalities have government agencies available to assist you with family information, referrals, and crises. Look in the telephone directory under the name of your city, county, or state for the address and telephone number of the agency you'd like to contact for more information. For general assistance in obtaining resources, information or assistance, contact the Social or Human Services Department, the Public Health Department, Youth Services Bureau, Community Rehabilitation Services or the Education Department in your community. Three additional agencies, the United Way, American Red Cross and the Salvation Army, provide various family services and provide excellent information for referrals which will address your particular parenting or overall family need.

On the national level, there are numerous departments and divisions that may provide the assistance you're looking for. To locate a particular agency, program or service, you should contact the closest Federal Information Center. The Federal Information Center (FIC) Program was established to provide one-stop sources of assistance for callers with inquiries about Federal agencies, programs, or services. Residents of seventy-two of the nation's key metropolitan areas call their FIC on a local-call basis; four states (Iowa, Kansas, Missouri, and Nebraska) can reach their FIC with a toll-free 800 number. A complete list of FIC telephone numbers and addresses is available in a descriptive brochure that may be requested by sending a postcard to Federal Information Center, Consumer Information Center, Pueblo, CO 81009.

•*Information centers.* Large cities usually have centers that can be called for specific child-rearing information. One such public service is Tel-Med, a free telephone health library for the public, available in over 340 cities in the United States, Canada and Venezuela. Tel-Med presently receives over one million calls each month and provides three- to five-minute prerecorded messages on over 500 topics, including stuttering/speech problems, first-aid for sprains, the proper use of prescription medicine, your baby's development, diabetes in children, brothers and sisters getting along, the single-parent family, puberty and adolescence, teenage alcoholism, and stress management. Check your telephone directory or write to Tel-Med Inc., 952 South Mt. Vernon Avenue, P.O. Box 1768, Colton, CA 92324. For more information, you can also call 714-825-6034.

Another national center, The Office of Disease Prevention and Health Promotion (ODPHP) National Health Information Center is a health information referral organization—they put people with health questions in touch with those organizations that are best able to answer them. Call toll-free 800-336-4797 (in Maryland call 301-565-4167).

•*Family Information Network Database (FIND).* The Guideposts Associates FIND program is a free, confidential service that gives individuals a personalized listing of agencies and programs relating to particular family interests or needs. FIND is one of the many outreach services offered to the general public through Guideposts Ministries and is supported by contributions to Guideposts.

The FIND program began in the summer of 1989 when I discovered a desperate need for a centralized comprehensive inventory of helping agencies to provide family help and information to troubled individuals. Checking with various agencies and verifying their programs and services, I began collecting names for a comprehensive database. FIND, as the list was called, grew to over 2,500 national and regional agencies and groups. To date, the FIND referral service has aided thousands of individuals in locating specific sources of assistance. Call Guideposts FIND toll-free at 800-233-0773.

Inspiration

•Inspirational phone recordings. Dial Guideposts for Inspiration is just one of the many inspirational programs and services available throughout the U.S. This service provides daily uplifting messages and a referral agency, if needed. It provides inspiration to almost one million callers every year and is available in twenty-six major U.S. cities and one in Canada (Winnipeg). To obtain a free bookmark listing the available numbers, write to Guideposts Associates, Inc., Dial Guideposts for Inspiration, 39 Seminary Hill Road, Carmel, NY 10512. Check your local telephone directory for other helpful, uplifting services (also see the next section)—these are great boosts to help you cope with difficult parenting and family situations.

Someone You Can Talk To

One of your most helpful options is to discuss their child-rearing concerns with someone else. Your objective may not always be to obtain advice or find an answer. You may simply be hoping to find someone who listens, really listens.

•*Friends and relatives.* It is always helpful to confide in a person who is close to you and who may understand your situation from your point of view.

•*Clergy.* If you take the initiative to contact a clergy member and feel comfortable talking with him or her, this can be a valuable parenting and personal resource.

•*National hotlines/helplines.* There are literally thousands of hotlines or helplines throughout the country. Many of them focus on a particular problem such as drugs, the homeless, runaways. One national service, known as CONTACT, covers all areas of the U.S., is confidential, and has trained volunteers on the lines to assist you. CONTACT began its first U.S. service in 1967 and was modeled after the Australian crisis intervention telephone ministry, Life Line International. CONTACT has more than seventy centers, nation-wide. To find the number of the closest center, write to CONTACT USA, Pouch A, Harrisburg, PA 17105 (or call 717-232-3501).

Complimentary Copy of the FIND Toll Free Number Directory. The Guideposts FIND Toll Free Number Directory is a listing of 450 toll-free numbers of helping agencies listed in the FIND database. It has been created to assist individuals and families in obtaining immediate assistance with their problems. The listing is organized by subject headings.
SEND FOR YOUR FREE FIND DIRECTORY BY RETURN-ING THE BUSINESS REPLY CARD IN THIS BOOK.

Helping Organizations for Parents

•*Here are some of the major U.S. hotline/helpline numbers offering toll-free personal help:*

Al-Anon Family Group Headquarters, Inc.	800-356-9996
Association of Jewish Family and Children's Agencies	800-634-7346
Beechnut Nutrition Hotline	800-523-6633
Beyond Rejection Ministries, Inc. (assistance for AIDS victims and families)	800-966-2437
Connecticut Parent Advocacy Center (CPAC)	800-445-2722
Covenant House (homes for runaways)	800-999-9999
Families Anonymous	800-736-9805
Family Service America	800-221-2681

Father Flanigan's Boys Town National Hotline
(counseling and referral service for parents
and troubled children)   800-448-3000
Focus on the Family   800-A-FAMILY
Gerber Hotline   800-4-GERBER
Mothers Without Custody   800-457-MWOC
National Committee for Citizens
in Education   800-638-9675
National Association for Family Day Care   800-359-3817
National Runaway Hotline   800-231-6946
Parents Without Partners   800-637-7974
Stepfamily Association of America   800-735-0329

Beware! Besides the toll-free 800 numbers, there are now many 900 numbers available for information and counseling. But these are pay numbers, with the charge ranging from $.75 to over $5.00 per minute. Be careful—know exactly what organization or group you are calling, what information you want, and what the charge will be.

•*Support groups.* There are many local and national child-rearing support groups throughout the country. Community agencies can help you find a group that will meet your particular needs. A complete listing of family-related groups is also available in *The Self-Help Sourcebook.* To obtain information and an order form, write Self-Help Clearinghouse, St. Clare's-Riverside Medical Center, Pocono Road, Denvill, NJ 07834.

One key national support group for parents is Parents Anonymous. This service provides resources and offers an 800 counseling number. Dial 800-421-0353 (or 800-352-0386 in California) and the Parents Anonymous national staff will provide you with the appropriate 800 number in your state (you can also check your telephone directory for your regional number).

Other support groups have proven to be helpful in many areas, including addictions, disabilities, illnesses, bereavement, and parenting concerns. Former U.S. Surgeon General C. Everett Koop expressed his view of support groups in this manner: "Curing and repairing are no longer enough...I believe in self-help as an effective way of dealing with problems, stress, hardship, and pain."

Professional Assistance

Make use of outside professional help as soon as you feel it is needed. Contact one or more of the following individuals:

•*Physicians*. Whenever physical or mental concerns arise within your family, a doctor or other qualified healthcare professional should be consulted.

•*School authorities*. Educational concerns should be addressed with your child's teacher, school administrators, and guidance counselors.

•*Professional counselors*. If you feel your parenting circumstances warrant the assistance of this a profession, make every effort to pursue this avenue and find a qualified counselor.

•*Law enforcement officials*. Although referring to this source of assistance is usually a last resort, remember that the police and related civil service employees are available for aid.

START IS: SHAPING TOMORROW'S ADULTS BY REACHING OUT TODAY

DAY 23 : START scheduling some time for yourself by participating in one of your favorite activities. You will become refreshed and rejuvenated.

Want Time for Yourself?

Adults enjoy adult companionship. As a parent, you will still want to keep social contacts with other adults. In fact, you need the company of other adults. Time with your friends is important and should be included in your daily or weekly schedule. Use the phone or get-togethers such as meals or shopping trips to keep in contact with friends and relatives. The other aspect of needing to be with adults is remembering your spouse or partner, if you have one. Raising a child can take attention and energy away from your relationship. To help avoid this, make sure you continue to spend focused time with that special person. Spend time together without your child to keep the relationship strong. Continue to share with each other your concerns, hopes, and dreams. And keep the relationship exciting—maybe even schedule time for a date each week!

Continue to enjoy your favorite activities, hobbies, and the sports you use to love to participate in, but remember that your participation may involve some changes.

•*Realization 1.* You cannot do all the things you used to do before you became a parent. There will be less time available for your interests if you are giving the needed attention and quantity time to raising your child. Time restraints will have a way of forcing you to set priorities. Realize this and pick your top five activities. My top five are hiking, racquetball or tennis, jogging, biking, and photography. I try to plan time for these activities without jeopardizing time with my family.

•*Realization 2.* It is helpful that your child knows that you enjoy a part of your life separate from her or him. This awareness assists in setting boundaries that are valuable to your child's growing independence and eventual need to separate.

Time for yourself is important, whether it be in the form of relaxation, exercise, solitude, socializing or participating in a favorite activity. Treat yourself to a break from your child and return to parenting with renewed enthusiasm.

Going the Extra Mile

Sign up for a class, a tournament, a seminar, or any activity that you enjoy. Bring a friend or a relative who has a similar interest.

Guidelines:

•Try a favorite activity or try something completely new.

•Make every effort to attend. Getting there may be the hardest part; but once you're there, you'll be glad you came.

• Share with your child your feelings about being away from the family and describe some of the activities you participated in. Be interested in what he or she did while you were away.

S T A R T IS: SHAPING TOMORROW'S ADULTS BY REACHING OUT TODAY

DAY 24 : START observing and evaluating the environment and people you leave your child with. Proper surroundings will give your child valuable learning experiences, and you will have greater peace of mind.

A Word about Leaving Your Children with Others

Whether it be for work, time to rest or an evening out, you will eventually look for child care or babysitters.

Nearly half of the U.S. infants and toddlers, more than half of America's preschool children, and two-thirds of its school-age children are entrusted daily to some form of supplementary outside-the-home care.[3]

If you are working full-time, you must understand the importance of researching the facility or home where you will leave your child. You will also be concerned about the background and experience of your child's care-givers. Parents are not simply buying a service here—they are selecting their child's primary waking environment! A major concern is safety, but there's much more to consider. Just as in your home environment, your child has needs that must be met if she or he is to feel at ease in these surroundings away from the home.

The board of directors of the Southern Association on Children Under Six (SACUS), a non-profit educational organization whose purpose is to work on behalf of young children and their families, takes the position that any child has certain fundamental needs that must be met in care:

• Your child needs to feel that the situation is a safe and comfortable place for her or him to be.

• Your child needs to learn to feel good about her- or himself.

• Your child needs to be fully employed in activities that are meaningful to her or him and that provide support in her or his full-time quest to learn.

• Your child needs to develop the ability to live comfortably with other children and adults.

• Your child needs to have her or his physical development supported and be helped to learn health, nutritional, and safety practices.

• Any child in care needs to feel that there is consistency in her or his life and a shared concern for her or his well-being among the important people in her or his life—parents and care-givers.[4]

If you need to leave your child with family, friends, a day care provider, or a child care center, thoroughly evaluate the situation and ask the following questions:

• Is the atmosphere safe, supportive, and caring?

• What are the disciplinary policies? Are they fair, consistent, and appropriate for young children?

• Is there a variety of activities and playthings—indoors and outdoors—for your child?

• Is the staff/person experienced and trained? Have minimum certification standards been met?

• Will your child be properly supervised? Most experts recommend a child-to-adult ratio of no more than 4:1 for infants; 5:1 for toddlers eighteen months to two years, 8:1 for children two to three years, 10:1 for three- to four-year-olds, 15:1 for children five to six years old, and 20:1 for children seven years and older.

• What size is the group of children your child will be with? Are there other children? Do you feel there are too many other children?

• Do you have some way of being contacted in the case of an emergency? Do you have a backup "emergency person" if you are unable to be reached?

•Are the center's facilities clean and well maintained? Is there a special area for sick children? Is proper hygiene a priority?

•Does the care-giver know your child? Will you be informed about your child's daily interests, behavior, and progress?

You as a parent need time alone or with other adults, and your child deserves the very best attention and care in your absence. The news is filled with too many horror stories of children who are left in the care of individuals who neglect or abuse. Do not entrust your child to someone before getting all the facts, taking time to observe the daily routine and the care premises, and getting recommendations from other parents. Taking the quantity time to find a qualified, loving individual or caring agency/facility is always worth the effort, both for you and for your child.

"We must always change, renew, rejuvenate ourselves; otherwise we harden."

—*Goethe*

CHAPTER

7

Children Learn What They Live

"Children need models more than they need critics."

—Joseph Joubert

My three-year-old son, Ryan, and I had just returned from the corner store. As always, Ryan checked to make sure that I had worn my seat belt during the entire trip. With a mandatory seat belt law in our state, Sue and I always try to make it a habit to wear our seat belts in the car. Besides the obvious safety issue, our wearing seat belts helps convince Ryan by example that he needs to "buckle up" in his car seat. When we returned home, Sue decided to go shopping. Ryan agreed with me that while she was away we would do some yardwork. After a quick good-bye to Mom, we ventured into the back yard. As Sue pulled out of the driveway, Ryan quickly ran through the front yard toward the road. Visions of horror flashed through my mind. But to my surprise and delight, Ryan stopped at the edge of the front lawn and bellowed, "Mom, put your seat belt on!"

I learned two lessons that day. One was that we shouldn't always expect the worst in a given situation. Children may surprise you with very positive action. More importantly, I realized that this was just another instance of how earnestly children model adult behavior. The importance of using a seat belt was firmly impressed on Ryan, and he was letting us know that.

Children Learn What They Live **137**

Parents who are trying to teach their children proper behavior should explain why a given conduct is appropriate or not, but it is the example set by the parent that makes a lasting impression. Your actions will substantiate what you say. As Oliver Goldsmith explains, "You can preach a better sermon with your life than your lips."

S T A R T IS: SHAPING TOMORROW'S ADULTS BY REACHING OUT TODAY

DAY 25 : START paying more attention to what you do than to what you preach. Children learn more by following examples than by verbal instructions.

It's Like Looking in a Mirror

Children learn a great deal by watching family, friends, and playmates. We parents are the first people that a child will imitate, as they subconsciously play the game of "monkey see, monkey do."

Esphyr Slobodkina's 1947 classic children's story, *Caps for Sale*, perfectly exemplifies this phrase. A cap peddler rests by a tree with his stack of caps. As he awakens, he discovers all his caps are missing but one, the one he is wearing. He quickly realizes that sixteen monkeys have taken the caps and are watching him from the tree above, all wearing his brown, green, gray, and red caps. The monkeys mimic his actions to get his caps back. The peddler shakes his finger; the monkeys each shake a finger. He stamps his feet; so do the monkeys. And so it goes until, thoroughly disgusted at his failure to retrieve the caps, the peddler throws the cap he is wearing to the ground and so do all the monkeys.

Whatever you do, whether it's good or bad, if it looks appealing or your child sees it on a consistent basis, your behavior will probably be imitated. Even your movements and facial expressions will be mimicked by your offspring; you may sometimes feel as though you're looking in a mirror.

While on vacation one summer, our family decided to go to Sesame Place in Langhorn, Pennsylvania, then to Great Adventure, a Six Flags theme park, and from there to visit the Jersey shore. At Great

Adventure, I could not help but observe other children and their parents walking around. One family in particular caught my attention. A mother loudly scolded her nine-year-old daughter, "You're not behaving very well. You did the same thing at Sesame Place. Stop yelling at your brother and sister!" It made me cringe to watch this scene because it was obvious where the daughter picked up this loud behavior.

How a child acts is usually a telltale sign of how a the parent acts. I've written the following piece to help illustrate this point:

Silent Approval

A father *borrowed* a computer software package from work to copy onto his home computer.

His son *stole* a Nintendo cartridge from a classmate to use at home.

A mother was talking about how a neighbor helped *adjust* the figures on her tax form to help her family's financial situation.

Her daughter *cheated* on her history exam by copying a friend's answers, hoping to improve her grade average.

The father *took* two extra pieces of wood at the lumber yard when he was loading his truck, just in case he needed them.

His son *pilfered* new baseballs from his Little League team, just in case he needed them.

The mother *selected* some fruit from the market and gave it to her child to eat while shopping—"It's a store benefit."

Her daughter *ripped off* an ice cream bar at her school at lunch time—"My parents pay school taxes."

The father *borrowed* a neighbor's car and accidentally put a scratch in the door and explained he was *unaware* of the damage.

His daughter *used* a friend's bike and bent the wheel rim and *accused* the other kids on the block.

The mother enjoyed going out for a cocktail or two every Friday after work to *socialize*.

Her daughter was invited to a party and *tried to be part of the gang* by drinking alcohol.

The son and daughter felt sure their parents would be very proud of them for they were following in their parents' footsteps and mirroring the examples their parents had set.

But the father and mother were disappointed in their children's actions. In their anger, they blamed their children's friends, the school system, and society for letting the children "turn out the way they did."

A parent's example is silent approval.

Your behavior and how you treat your child will determine to a great extent how he or she will respond to the world and conduct his or her interpersonal relationships in the future. Although this behavioral concept may be simple to comprehend and hard to dispute, parents must make a constant, conscious effort to model positive behavior for their children.

START IS: SHAPING TOMORROW'S ADULTS BY REACHING OUT TODAY

DAY 26 : START treating your child as you would like to be treated—the Golden Rule is alive and well! If your actions reflect this attitude, you will foster mutual consideration and respect.

Do You Want a Child Who?

Your actions and reactions will help your child formulate his or her self-image and gain greater understanding of the world. Most of this mirroring takes place during the times of day when a child and parent routinely interact: in the morning, after school, and at bedtime.

My wife and I made an extra effort to be friendly, caring, and considerate to our first child, Ryan. Hugs, kisses, and positive feedback were actions that became priorities and everyday requirements for us. Similar responses from Ryan were openly received, but not expected. When Zachary was born, we were pleased to see Ryan's open and loving response to his new baby brother. Ryan gave out abundant hugs and kisses in the early weeks, followed by an active interest and participation in Zachary's daily needs and special events such as his baptism. As Zachary grew, Ryan took a special interest in protecting him from handling small toy parts that might be harmful to him. We gave Ryan a device to assist him in this mission, a No-Choke tube. This small tube (available from Toys to Grow On, P.O. Box 17, Long Beach, CA 90801) allows Ryan to test each small plaything to see if it is safe for Zachary.

Ryan's concern to protect and care for others was not instilled in him in one day or even in one month. Values are learned by a child from birth and throughout childhood. By consistently displaying fundamental moral principles, you will be gratified to see that your child will learn what he or she lives.

Take a moment to think about what you want your child to be like. Do you want a child who:

> Is friendly and has the ability to love, or a child who is hostile to others?

> Likes him- or herself, or feels self-pity?

> Is patient and has faith in others, or criticizes and condemns others?

> Has peace of mind, or feels guilty?

> Is appreciative and generous, or is envious?

> Strives toward a goal, or is apprehensive?

> Is confident, or is shy?

> Knows what truth and justice are, or lies and cheats?

Dorothy Law Nolte provides a powerful parenting guide with this familiar poem.

Children Learn What They Live

If a child lives with criticism, he learns to condemn.

If a child lives with hostility, he learns to fight.

If a child lives with fear, he learns to be apprehensive.

If a child lives with pity, he learns to feel sorry for himself.

If a child lives with ridicule, he learns to be shy.

If a child lives with jealousy, he learns what envy is.

If a child lives with shame, he learns to feel guilty.

If a child lives with encouragement, he learns to be confident.

If a child lives with tolerance, he learns to be patient.

If a child lives with praise, he learns to be appreciative.

If a child lives with sharing, he learns to be generous.

If a child lives with acceptance, he learns to love.

If a child lives with approval, he learns to like himself.

If a child lives with recognition, he learns it is good to have a goal.

If a child lives with honesty and fairness, he learns what truth and justice are.

If a child lives with security, he learns to have faith in himself and in those around him.

If a child lives with friendliness, he learns that the world is a nice place in which to live.

If you live with serenity, your child will live with peace of mind.

A Few Minutes Are Very Important

When family members are apart and reunite at the end of a day or ein the morning after a night's rest, the first four minutes—many times the first minute—set the mood for subsequent family interactions.

There's a familiar story about how a CEO in a large corporation was having a horrendous day that consisted of work delays, employee problems, and continuous interruptions. Frustrated and angry, he passed this mood down to his manager, who in turn reacted in a similar manner. The manager's negative attitude was transmitted to his administrative assistant. By this time, it was the end of the day. The administrative assistant went home "boiling mad" and displaced this anger onto her child. The child, unaware of this circulation of negative feelings at the office, was surprised and confused. Almost immediately, the child developed the same frame of mind, and he kicked the cat in an effort to vent his feelings. And if no animal had been present, a sibling or the other parent would have become the recipient of this unnecessary backlash.

The point is not that a child should be protected against strong feelings, but that a child should be told that your mood has nothing to do with his or her behavior.

The attitude, mood, and the manner in which you greet your family is so important. Even if you've had a terrible day, try to set aside those feelings of irritation and rage during your initial interaction with your family. Work problems have nothing to do with your family, so try to put them aside and focus on your child; your good cheer will be contagious. By placing key importance on that first interaction when you walk through the door each evening, you can effect a much more relaxed atmosphere, closer family feelings, and a better evening all around.

Metaphorically speaking, if the song you sing is positive, and you are aware of the words, the tone, and the method of your delivery, your child will sing the same sweet tune. Aware parents who want their kids to develop secure, self-confidant personalities, with an ability to love and a deep sense of self-respect and worth, must "ac-cen-tu-ate the positive" whenever possible.[1]

Negative remarks you make today can damage your child's self-image forever.

It happened more than fifteen years ago. I was taking a school elective in photography. I was very interested in photography, both technically and artistically, and the class promised instruction from both perspectives. For our first assignment I enthusiastically set out to capture the beautiful Hudson Valley in pictures. My passion was quickly squelched. The instructor not only critiqued my work harshly, but belittled me personally, killing any interest I had in further pursuing this hobby.

With sincere support from family and friends, my passion for photography was rekindled. I have developed some expertise in this area and have used it extensively at work and for fun. For me, Carl Buchner spoke the truth when he wrote, "They (children) may forget what you said but they'll never forget how you made them feel."

An event may be important to your child, but it's the emotions that he or she experiences that have a greater effect. Every day, find an opportunity to give praise and encouragement to your child instead of criticism. Whenever you praise your child, strive to give immediate and specific praise. For instance, telling a child you appreciated his help in cleaning up the table is more meaningful than, "You are a good boy." Along with praise, encouragement provides a child with specific knowledge and positive feedback on his or her strengths and abilities and allows him to feel good about him- or herself.

The following is a poem that shows two different approaches to a child who has tried his best:

I Got Two A's Today

"I got two A's," the small boy said.
His voice was filled with glee.
His father very bluntly asked,
"Why didn't you get three?"

"Mom, I've got the dishes done,"
The girl called from the door.
Her mother very calmly said,
"Did you sweep the floor?"

"I mowed the grass," the tall boy said.
"And put the mower away."
His father asked him with a shrug,
"Did you clean off the clay?"

The children in the house next door
Seemed happy and content.
The same things happened over there,
But this is how it went:

"I got two A's," the small boy said.
His voice was filled with glee.
His father very proudly said, "That's great;
I'm glad you belong to me."

"Mom, I've got the dishes done,"
The girl called from the door.
Her mother smiled and softly said,
"Each day I love you more."

"I mowed the grass," the tall boy said.
"And put the mower away."
His father answered with much joy,
"You've made my happy day."

Children deserve a little praise
For tasks they're asked to do.
If they're to lead a happy life,
So much depends on you.[2]

Going the Extra Mile

Don't take your child for granted. Express sincere appreciation to your child, at an appropriate time this week, as you would to your partner, co-worker, or boss. Realize that every child wears an invisible sign that says, "Please help me feel good about myself!"

Guidelines:

- Express true feelings; a child easily detects false appreciation.

- Give a compliment or praise without any anticipation of a return compliment.

- Look for the best in your child *on a regular basis*.

What Motivates a Child's Actions?

As your child grows, his or her behavior is motivated by a number of factors including a r*eward, a leader, a purpose, recognition, the need to belong, the promise of a pleasant experience, or the avoidance of an unpleasant one*. As a parent you should be aware of these motivating forces and take a major role in effecting positive results in your child's behavior.

- Your child is motivated by simple *rewards* such as your attention, your approval, your smile, and your praise. Children want parents to like them. When parents show them that they do, children feel good about themselves. This kind of reward is very meaningful and it has a long-term positive effect. As your child grows, he or she will begin to realize that people also recognize material rewards as important and will request these in various forms. Assist your child in recognizing a healthy, balanced picture of the function and role of *material* rewards in society. In a family setting, this type of reward may take the form of a special privilege, like going to a movie on a Friday night with Mom and Dad or getting tickets to a special event. As your child continues to grow, you should be a major factor in providing rewards, with an emphasis on you providing ongoing verbal appreciation to your child, continuous sharing of your time and attention,and displaying actions that reinforce positive behavior.

•A *leader* can be you, a neighbor, a relative, a coach, a teacher—someone to look up to, a role model to follow.

•A *purpose* for your child may consist of an activity he or she wants to complete, somewhere he or she wants to go, or a task he or she feels strongly about completing. If the activity is constructive, by all means encourage your child to pursue it. Give your child the needed support to achieve a goal without "taking over." Take time to recognize your child's efforts and accomplishment.

•*Recognition* can be bestowed in the forms of praise, affection, or attention. Or consider giving your child a trophy, plaque, ribbon, special meal, or party.

•The *need to belong* can be met by friends, classmates, or teammates. Fulfill this need in the family setting by making your child's home life a "safe refuge" that is both challenging and fun. Encourage a sense of community by joining religious groups, attending town and school functions, and entertaining your extended family and friends.

•Your child will expend a great deal of energy to accomplish something that is wanted. If something is *enjoyable*, your child will be easily motivated to participate. An *unpleasant experience* can provide motivation, too. Neglect, abuse, and a negative home environment can motivate a child to search for recognition, a sense of belonging and more pleasing experiences elsewhere, as I discovered with a boy named Michael.

While still in college, I had the opportunity to complete my field work in a city housing project. My responsibility was to offer recreational activities to children after school. Most of the activities I presented were active ones, since I realized that after a full day of school children need to release the energy they've stored up during the day. While playing a variety of tag and ball games, a small boy named Michael (6) came over to where I was sitting to rest awhile. Michael was a very affectionate boy who was willing to share his feelings openly. He told me that his older brother was on the playground with his friends, and sometimes they didn't let Michael play with them because he was too young. He was disappointed about that, but he quickly rebounded by saying how happy he was to find a new friend—me!

The following five times I returned to the housing project, Michael was very exuberant about having me come and visit. He spent a great deal of time and energy trying to gain my individual attention for the majority of the afternoon. Michael was obviously looking for attention, approval and friendship, and he was highly motivated in his search for these responses. I later found out that Michael's home life was poor. During my last session at the center I was very sorry to leave, knowing that Michael, who had reached out to a stranger to establish a relationship, might try to fulfill his needs in a much less constructive way.

Michael yearned to feel important, and so does your child. Take advantage of opportunities to fill this need within your family before your child is motivated to search elsewhere.

The Process and Value of Choosing

Everyone likes to have a choice. Even if it is limited, the power of choice is an important aspect of commitment. If people make a choice, they will enjoy the selection or follow through on the decision much more than if no options were offered. This is true at work, school, play, and home.

Here's an example of the power of choice for our son, Ryan. It was more than a train set. It was a toy town that included people, trees, houses, cars—even miniature swimming pools and a gazebo. During a winter evening at home, Ryan requested that we get some of the set out of storage, in particular all the people, cars, and houses. My reply was, "Sure I can take it out for you—with the understanding that you will be cleaning it up after you finish playing." My son's enthusiastic response was, "I will. I will. Let's get it out now." I brought in the three boxes of "goodies" from the garage, and Ryan thoroughly enjoyed dumping the boxes out and setting up a small town. As the evening went on, it was getting near bedtime, which meant clean-up time. Although he obviously was ready to go to bed, Ryan was not in any great hurry to clean up. It became decision time for Ryan. I made the choice clear for him: "Clean up or you will not be playing with these toys again." This was not said as a threat but more as a clarification of what was understood before these toys were brought out. After some moaning and groaning, Ryan decided it was worth cleaning up this time.

When the opportunity is available and appropriate, make use of an important two-letter word—*or*. Use it at mealtime corn *or* beans; when getting dressed—blue *or* green shirt; before doing homework—spelling *or* math first. Focusing on this power of choice accomplishes your goal (getting a task done) and helps your child learn to make decisions and gain confidence in the process. Your child is becoming an individual and needs opportunities for self-expression. Making choices will help her or him define interests and assert individuality.

Discipline

One of the most popular adult classes in our community is dog-obedience class. One Tuesday evening I had to drop off a revised roster for the instructor. I stayed awhile to observe the instructor's techniques. An owner was having difficulty with her dog. The dog continually jumped up on people. It was a good sized "mutt" and very friendly. The instructor, who looked pleased about this teaching opportunity, stood up facing the dog and coaxed him to jump on her. As the dog jumped up, the instructor kneed the dog right in the chest. The dog fell to the floor, stunned and out of breath. The instructor called the dog again. The dog jumped up and was immediately kneed into the chest again, yelping as he fell. The instructor tried a third time. The dog did not come, instead heading in the opposite direction. The dog did learn what was expected in this situation, but he was obeying out of fear, not respect. Some parents treat their children in a similar fashion. If a parent uses verbal abuse and physical punishment for disciplining, it is as if the parent is kneeing the child right in the chest.

To many, discipline means judgment, punishment, and penalties. But discipline can be positive and take the everyday form of praise, making a child feel important, being consistent, offering appropriate and attainable challenges, enforcing limits and boundaries, instilling trust, and providing opportunities for growth.

If your child misbehaves or you feel his or her actions are inappropriate, a good helpful first step to take is to count to ten, then think "COUNT."

C = *Control and courtesy*. Control yourself and your actions. Be courteous; every child and adult deserves respect.

O = *Opportunities*. Recognize that discipline provides a variety of opportunities, to set the example by what you say and do, to involve your child in family decisions and discussions, to teach proper behavior (be specific in clarifying your expectations), and to listen to your child's thoughts and feelings.

U = *Understanding*. Try to understand your child's feelings. Is your child angry, scared, excited, frustrated, or is he or she feeling pressured? Also work to understand the present situation. Why is your child acting this way? Does he or she want attention or added independence; is your child tired, hungry, or sick?

N = *Negotiate*. Ask yourself, can I be flexible in this situation or should I be firm? Can I say "No" in a way that means "I love you?"

T = *Talk and touch*. Whatever takes place, express your love for your child in some form, whether verbally or physically. Give something that relieves tension, combats depression, reduces stress, improves circulation, and has no unpleasant side effects—a hug, of course.

Counting to ten is a mini timeout for you to remain controlled, composed, and give some thought to your actions. A similar timeout for your child is just as effective.

"Just This One Time"

In the first years of life, a child learns from whatever he or she is allowed to do. As a parent, you may find yourself in a given situation in which your actions do not reflect your convictions. You say to yourself, "I'll only do it just this one time." A common everyday example of this is when a parent brings a supermarket cart full of groceries to the register. The child is restlessly grabbing everything within arm's reach, including a candy bar. The parent's immediate response is "No." The child screams. The parent who normally would not give a candy bar to the child "on demand," does so this time to quiet the child. The parent thinks, "Just this one time." What happens the next time they go grocery shopping? Most likely it will be a reenactment of the prior scene, at least on the child's part. Why? Because if you do it once, a child expects it to be done again. For the child it has become a routine: "As we go through the check-out line, I will get a candy bar."

What are your alternatives?

First, you should stand firm on what you want to do. In the supermarket example, do not give your child a candy bar. This may be uncomfortable for the moment because your child may "make a scene," a loud one. But most likely your child will understand what will take place the next time. Think of the value in the long run.

The second option is to be prepared for potential discipline problems. Have a toy from home or a healthy snack ready when you go through the check-out line. Essentially, provide your child with an alternative in any particular situation.

Reinforcing behavior can be used in a positive manner, whether it be hugs and kisses each time you depart, saying grace at a mealtime, cleaning up one game before playing another, and using "please" and "thank you." By repetition and consistency (if you do it once, a child expects it to be done again), children learn to anticipate appropriate behavior.

Boundaries and Rules

Two of the most popular children's games are hide-'n-seek and kickball. Before playing either one, children must select teams or choose an "it" and review the rules and boundaries. They discuss what is "out of bounds" and what is "fair."

Children readily understand and need guidelines. They quickly comprehend that there are rules and limits to what they can do. It is the obligation of parents to provide this framework. Parents need to define boundaries with kindness, understanding, and without harsh character judgment.

Four factors to consider when you are establishing "rules and boundaries" with your child are:

1. Whenever possible include your child in setting up the rules and deciding what the repercussions will be if they are broken.

2. Depending on your child's age, provide the reasoning behind your rules and consequences. The better he or she understands why something is done, the more likely the rule will be followed. A child likes to know what is going on, and he or she will feel recognized and important when you take the time to explain.

4. Be consistent yet flexible. Do the new rules relate to previous rules and decisions that you've made? Do they make sense? This does not mean that rules cannot be changed. On the contrary, there should be flexibility. Changing life situations and age differences may be reasons to adopt revisions.

As your child grows up, you will need to review and modify his or her responsibilities and privileges, sometimes by necessity and sometimes by choice. Chores, selection of clothes, style of hair, use of make-up, time spent with friends, amount of television viewing, and extended bedtimes are but a few issues that you will have to re-evaluate on a continuous basis with your child.

S T A R T IS: SHAPING TOMORROW'S ADULTS BY REACHING OUT TODAY

DAY 27 : START "being there" for your growing child. Provide the support and challenges to fulfill your child's changing needs and interests. Your genuine interest, and quantity time, creates a trusting and lasting relationship.

Challenges

One cool Saturday in September, two boys from our neighborhood, ages nine and ten, didn't know quite what to do. It seemed baseball was over, it was too cool to go swimming, and it was apparent that the boys were bored. The woods at the edge of town lead to a nearby apple orchard, which is privately owned. The boys decided to spend some time in the woods on their way to their final destination, the orchard.

Later that afternoon, one of the boys came up to me holding a box of about twenty-five apples, and he asked me if I would like to buy some. I asked where he got the apples and he honestly and proudly explained, "We went to the apple orchard and picked them!" I declined the offer. The following day I saw one of the boys in his yard playing ball and I noticed that his face looked swollen. I asked what had happened. He explained that while playing in the woods and climbing trees, he had rubbed against poison ivy. By evening his parents had had to take him to the emergency room with a very bad case of poison ivy. I joked with him and said, "I bet the next time you won't take any more apples." He nodded.

In this case, the boys learned a lesson. But many times when children go looking for an activity that is exciting or challenging, it may involve something that is mischievous or in "bad taste." As children develop, they start to crave adventure and new challenges. Be alert to when your child seems to step up to a new level of boldness. This provides an opportunity for building added confidence if your child's energies and renewed spirit are directed to appropriate endeavors.

Supporting Growth

Children are dependent upon adults for direction, approval, and love, but children also need freedom to assert their independence and to grow. Parents need to develop a kind of sensitivity to age, an openness to their child's needs, and an awareness of the dynamics of growth and of the way children respond to and use freedom.[3]

The Portland Adventist Elementary School has an interesting motto on its letterhead: "Children, the seeds of today . . . give them room to grow."

Gardening is a good metaphor for child-rearing. It can be interesting, enjoyable, and extremely fulfilling, but it also requires a great deal of attention and hard work. Tomato plants are probably the number-one vegetable planted in home gardens. Young tomato plants are usually purchased and placed in a small hole outdoors in a sunny area. After a few weeks of proper nourishment, sun, and water in good amounts, the plants grow to a size where they should be staked. The reason? In order to grow to its fullest potential and bear the best fruit, a tomato plant needs strong support. If the tomatoes touch the ground, the chances of decay and spoilage are greatly increased.

The same principle applies to your growing child. During the early growing stages, much attention, care, nourishment and protection is needed. As your child matures, he or she needs freedom to grow, as well as strong support. Your fruitful harvest will be a well-balanced, caring individual. Provide attention and nourishment, along with continuous support, throughout your child's life. It's essential!

§ T A R T IS: SHAPING TOMORROW'S ADULTS BY REACHING OUT TODAY

DAY 28 : START strengthening the traits needed for raising your child, including patience, understanding, flexibility, trust, and, especially, love. Cultivating these traits will improve all your relationships.

Parenthood Requirements

What are some of the traits needed for being a "good enough" parent? Think of traits as links in a chain. The stronger the links and the longer the chain, the stronger the bond and the parent-child relationship. Here's my list of required traits:

• Patience—the backbone of raising children. Patience is remembering that a child is new to this world and will be learning a great deal, including skills, values, feelings and behaviors—and that you are the teacher.

• Love—the river in you that will not run dry; the source for all patience.

• Stamina—the force that takes over when your "get up and go just got up and went." It's holding on during those tough days until you can have that "quiet time" when the children have gone to bed.

• Tolerance—the intricate combination of patience, love, and stamina.

•Understanding—the step beyond tolerance; tolerance with an abundance of love.

•Ability to Listen—your gateway to understanding.

•Being Realistic—knowing your physical and mental limits and when to ask for help.

•Self-control—the gear that needs to be engaged before your limit is reached.

•Flexibility—one of the forks in the road that enables you to bend rather than break when a crisis arises.

•Trust—the strength to reach out to someone else for assistance.

•Consistency—the trait you need when it comes to setting an example and providing discipline.

•Creativity—the realization that there are many options and opportunities available to you and your child in everyday situations.

•Common Sense—knowing when to be consistent or creative in any situation.

•Togetherness—sharing the good times as well as the difficult ones.

•Joy—enjoying the special moments, which helps you realize that what you are doing counts.

•Energy—essential for growing up with your children and capturing the joyful times.

•Wisdom—relying on your personal characteristics to provide the love, strength, and proper action for each parenting situation.

•Honesty—using your wisdom to be truthful in all you say and do with a child.

•Sincerity—the right combination of honesty and understanding.

•Generosity—heaping portions of love and quantity time for your child.

•Peace—the feeling each day that comes from knowing that you have given the amounts of love and time to your children to the best of your ability.

- Faith—knowing that the time and love you have given will produce a strong relationship and help your child become a well-balanced adult.

And the Greatest of These is Love

How can love be described? *Webster's Third International Dictionary* describes love as "the attraction, desire, or affection felt for a person who arouses delight or admiration or elicits tenderness, sympathetic interests, or benevolence.[4]

Probably the most descriptive and meaningful definition of love is from the Bible. Many are familiar with 1 Corinthians 13:4-7,13 as it is frequently included in wedding vows:

"Love is very patient and kind, never jealous or envious, never boastful or proud, never haughty or selfish or rude. Love does not demand its own way. It is not irritable or touchy. It does not hold grudges and will hardly even notice when others do it wrong. It is never glad about injustice, but rejoices whenever truth wins out. If you love someone you will be loyal to him no matter what the cost. You will always believe in him, always expect the best of him, and always stand your ground in defending him. There are three things that remain—faith, hope, and love—and the greatest of these is love."[5]

Sometimes in parenting it's hard to "see the forest for the trees." While we were finishing dinner one night, one of my sons kept opening and closing the porch screen door. This behavior was not wrong, just irritating. I began to think of all the parenting programs I had been evaluating in the past month and trying to decide which method I should use to rectify the situation. Mentally exhausted, I went through the pros and cons of Parent Effectiveness Training (PET), Systematic Training for Effective Parenting (STEP), The Next STEP, Active Parenting, and Family Talk. Meanwhile, my wife demonstrated the obvious approach I needed to be reminded of, and the answer to my parenting dilemma. Sue quietly took my son to his room, resolved his inappropriate behavior by participating in a two-way conversation, and capped off their exchange with a hug and a kiss.

A Child Knows

Children have an uncanny ability to comprehend the degree of sincerity behind an adult's expression of affection, interest, and consideration. We are the center of our children's worlds and they rely on us to make sense of their experiences and perception. How we act or react, what we say or do not say, and all our non-verbal cues are the focus of their attention.

One of our neighbors has ALS (Amoyotrophic Lateral Sclerosis), also known as Lou Gehrig's disease. Since this disease causes progressive muscle weakness and paralysis, he has great difficulty talking. Although his wife and two children have learned sign language, the other children in our neighborhood have not. Communication can be difficult at times. But one thing that is always communicated is his genuine interest in children and what they do. They can sense and feel his warmth and love. His smile, hand shakes, hugs, and participation in their games convey his sincere interest in them. Without words he demonstrates his feelings, which the children understand, experience, and appreciate. In return he receives their consideration and respect.

If children can sense true feelings just by actions, imagine how much more powerful verbal communication can be. Coaches, teachers, and, most of all, parents, must become aware of the great impact words—and silence—can have. Remember, a child knows . . . .

"There is no greater invitation to love than loving first."

—*St. Augustine of Hippo*

CHAPTER

Love Is Spelled T-I-M-E

"My definition of success is living a life that makes a difference. The question to ask is whether or not the world is a better place because of your efforts."

—Joan Ganz Cooney

START IS: SHAPING TOMORROW'S ADULTS BY REACHING OUT TODAY

DAY 29 : START taking care of finding the right balance in your life for work, family, and leisure. Harmony is the principal factor in achieving success.

On returning from a business trip to Atlanta some years ago, I was driving on the New York State Thruway from Laguardia Airport, heading north to go home. It was late, I was tired, and I knew I had to be cautious. To my surprise, the car ahead of me came to an abrupt stop from a fifty-miles-per-hour speed. I quickly swerved to the left lane and avoided a rear-end collision. As I passed the car, I noticed that the driver and passenger were both trying to locate the proper exit by attempting to read the overhead road sign. I was furious at their dangerous decision to stop in the middle of the highway.

As I continued to drive north, I realized that I, too, had come to an abrupt stop—not on the highway, but in my life. Sue and I were at a point in our marriage where we were ready to start a family. As we began to plan for the future, I realized I needed to reconsider my work schedule. I was working fifty to sixty hours a week, including weekends, and I was on call from 5:00 a.m. to 1:00 a.m. I decided to leave this job for a more stable and consistent work schedule, even if it would be less lucrative. I had stopped abruptly to read a road sign in my life. It said "FAMILY," and I needed to take the appropriate exit.

At that time, my career decision was not an easy one, but looking back, it was a major step toward raising my two sons in an atmosphere that stressed the importance of my family. That decision has allowed me to grow with my family, not watch them grow up from a distance.

When you become responsible for another human being, a child, decisions in your life become more difficult. As a parent, you must continuously examine and explore the various options available for yourself and your family members. When you're single, your focus can solely be on yourself, but now others are relying on you for support and nurturing.

A Growing Family

This kind of life re-evaluation—of career goals, financial status, adequate living space—needs to take place before you decide to have a second child. Additional children can bring added stress or added strength to the family unit. More is not always better if you're not well prepared. You need to be prepared physically (as in the health of the conceiving mother), financially (the ability to provide for the needs of an additional child), and mentally (to be aware of the thoughts and feelings of your partner, yourself, and your other children). If the parents have a positive attitude about adding another family member, chances are good that the children will, too. In the case of children, the right attitude is not so much taught, as caught. Parents need to set the tone for the rest of the family.

Before you decide to expand your family, you and your partner should be attuned to the following:

• Consider your existing child's growth and needs.

• Outline your needs as individuals (children, partner, yourself) and as a family.

Be sure to discuss the changes that would be taking place and their effects. As your family expands, each person must make home life more comfortable and enjoyable. Each person's contribution to family life should be recognized as important. Early relationships in a child's life will provide a strong foundation for the future. The family should be a major source of strength throughout your child's life.

A New Dimension

A growing family adds a new dimension to your child's life—siblings. New concerns arise, such as whether or not you can love your second child as much as your first and what kind of relationship will develop between your two children. Both concerns are valid and need to be addressed. If you are open to the changes to come in your family relationships and can accept added commitments in your already busy schedule, then you can resolve these issues.

You will also need to continue a positive approach to parenting. Keep repeating the affirmation, "I'm doing my best as a parent." Repeat the affirmation regularly; believe it and strive to better yourself as a well-informed, loving parent.

As for enough love, how much love can an adult provide a child? An unlimited amount. Norma Claypool is living proof. Norma adopted ten handicapped children in a span of twenty-one years. This feat alone is truly spectacular. But Norma is blind and has been since the age of two. She has not let her disability come in the way of loving her ten children. She provides for all their needs, and she lavishes the care and attention required for their development.

"I know a lot of people wonder how I manage, but it's really just a matter of having priorities. My kids come first—always.

"Every child has a right to a home and a quality life and a family's love while they're here.

"You know, I've often thought it is a blessing in disguise that I'm blind. Most people adopt children with their eyes. I adopt them with my heart.

"They're still human beings, no matter how handicapped or disfigured or retarded. They're still children." [1]

Another vital concern is the child-child relationship that develops when your family grows. Anyone who comes from a family with more than one child knows there are times when you "can't stand" your brother or sister and other times when he or she is your closest friend and companion. Betty Jo Connor of Chattanooga, Tennessee, a mother of two children, describes an experience that captures the genuine closeness that can develop between siblings.

"Time to go," I call to our three-year-old Sean—time to pick our second-grader, Nikki, up from school. Sean comes running to the car.

He loves to be with her, but oh, how he torments her. Nikki is always complaining about having her privacy invaded, about how Sean takes her things, her candy, her markers and never stops trying to horn in on her friends. And I well remember how his arrival shattered the calm world she had known as an only child.

At school, Nikki jumps into the car, closing the door. She turns and looks at her "monster" brother beside her in the backseat. "Mom," she announces, "he's asleep."

"Shhh," I respond, looking in the rearview mirror.

There he is in his car seat, his head drooped forward, the winter sun glinting on his tousled hair. He clutches a golf ball in one hand, and his pink ears poke out from beneath his blue hood. A coat zipper imprint runs like a railroad track from his cheek to his chin.

I ease into our driveway. Sean is still asleep and Nikki starts to climb out. She pauses to look at him again, the little brother she calls a "creep," a "spoiled brat," a "pest", and a "pain in the neck."

Gently, she leans over and kisses him.

The little brother she loves.[2]

Whether you have one child or six, your family will be the most important institution in your children's development. Do everything within your power to enable them to experience growth, reassurance, trust, and intimacy at home.

What is a Family?

In writing this book, I've come across much research and many opinions on the family of the past, today's family, and the structure and needs of tomorrow's family. In the preceding chapters, I've taken the opportunity to relive parts of my childhood and, hopefully, help you recall meaningful family experiences of your past—circumstances and events that have shaped your life.

A special edition of *Newsweek* focused on the twenty-first-century family, and the emphasis was on the changing family. What is a family today?

A family has many functions including maintaining the physical health and safety of its members, helping shape a belief system of goals and values, teaching social skills, and creating a place for recuperation from external stresses. But most importantly a family is "a group who love and care for each other.[3]

If love and caring exists in a family, a deep bond can form. Edith Schaffer expands on his in her book, *What Is a Family?*

A family is a mobile strung together with invisible threads—delicate, easily broken at first, growing stronger through the years, in danger of being worn thin at times, but strengthened again with special care. A family—blended, balanced, growing, changing, never static, moving with a breath of wind—babies, children, young people, mothers, fathers, grandparents, aunts, uncles—held in a balanced framework by the invisible threads of love, memories, trust, loyalty, compassion, kindness in honor, preferring each other, looking to each other for help, giving each other help, picking each other up, suffering long with each other's faults, understanding each other more and more, hoping all things, enduring all things, never failing! Continuity! Thin, invisible threads turning into thin, invisible metal that holds great weights but gives freedom of movement—a family![4]

The essential message I've stressed is to look at this bond between parent and child and how it can be formed. The strength of a family lies in the commitment to express your love openly and to share quantity time with your child today.

DAY 30 : START being a loving parent, grandparent, teacher, child care worker, neighbor, or friend by spending time with a child. Two people will be better for the effort—you and the child. The future of our children depends on you spending quantity time with them!

What Is a Family?

A family is a close-knit circle of loving people. Love in a family is a special blend of affection, devotion, and admiration displayed in the form of TIME.

TIME to share both the pleasurable activities and the challenging episodes life offers.

TIME to build each other up by sincere appreciation and by believing and encouraging each other to achieve personal dreams and goals.

TIME for forgiving and a continuous focus on caring for each other, in spite of any misgivings.

TIME for closeness—physical, emotional, social, and spiritual—with a child as he or she grows, and with lasting closeness as the child becomes an adult, cherishing childhood memories and continuing to share lifetime activities.

Family members are generous indeed. Not so much in the form of money and material possessions, but in designating TIME for each other TODAY.

Going the Extra Mile

Raising your family will evoke many thoughts and feelings. You may wish to remember these and reflect upon them at a later date. A journal or diary is a useful record of your parenting experiences. It provides an opportunity to capture memories, insights, joys, and statements of personal goals. Writing a diary also helps you cope with everyday family concerns and difficulties. Journaling provides time for reflection and a time for personal feelings to surface. It helps clarify your priorities and, as your children grow older, sharing the journal may be significant to everyone. See Chapter 9 for use of the START journal.

Guidelines:

• Write frequently (daily if possible).

• Choose a journaling time that is convenient—early morning, evening, or even break times at work. Dedicate fifteen to thirty minutes for each writing session.

• Include the positive and the negative and freely discuss your goals and feelings.

(Note: Having your child keep a journal can be very helpful and rewarding, too. Entries may include stories, pictures, and poems. Give your child the opportunity to start a journal, a great activity for both boys and girls.)

It's Never Too Late

Its never to late to start. Start setting aside and enjoying quantity time with your family. Making family time a personal priority is a process that you need to focus on today. It involves a commitment on your part. You need to take the initiative. Here are some helpful tips to consider:

•*Set your priorities.* There's a children's song that helps them realize what's important in their lives. It is a very simple song that allows the child to "fill in the blank." What would you put in the blank? I hope your children are very high on the list:

What is important,

That's what I want to know.

What is important,

Tell me if you know._____, _____, _____ is important.

I tell you and it's so.[5]

•*Make time for your child.* You have learned where you are spending your time and where adjustments can be made. Timesavers? Use them. Discover new ones. Time-wasters? Be aware of them. Control them. Whatever the case, make the time for your child because your child needs you. Cherish your time together.

•*Achieve success.* Children present us with a great opportunity to succeed as parents. You have an opportunity to provide an atmosphere of love, acceptance and trust for your child, along with experiences for discovery and growth. You will feel satisfaction when you give something of yourself. Impart to your child your enthusiasm and dedication.

•*Keep balance in your life.* Of course your job is important. So are chores, education, and time for yourself, yet you should know where your primary focus is and be in control of it. You are the one who best knows your goals and dreams.

I thought I might have "bitten off more than I could chew" when I signed up for an undergraduate calculus class (a prerequisite for entering the Masters program in Computer Science). The class would meet twelve straight weekday nights, three hours a night. This was only my second class after returning to school from an eight-year hiatus, and now I had the additional responsibilities of a full-time job and a family. It was obvious I needed to take some vacation days to complete the work for my class. I was juggling work, class, homework and study, time with my family, meals, sleep, and exercise (I knew I was going to need it).

For sixteen days, which included the weekends, it was hectic, but I felt I had balanced my time well. I was home at least four half-days, enjoyed two racquetball matches, went jogging, ate meals with the family, split firewood and stacked it, built three snowmen with Ryan, and I received an A in the course. My intensive program worked for that time, though I realized that this kind of schedule could not be sustained. In sixteen days I came to understand the difficulty of maintaining a balance and attempting to achieve "too much."

Be aware of your schedule, your organizational skills, your tolerance level, your needs and, most important, your family's needs. To maintain good balance in your life, use this four-step process daily:

1. Set your priorities.
2. Make time for your child.

3. Achieve success.

4. Keep balance in your life.

And as you arrange your time priorities, ask yourself three important questions:

1. Am I being fair to my child?

2. Am I being fair to my partner/mate?

3. Am I being fair to myself?

To a Loving Parent

When you become a first-time parent, friends and relatives tend to give you a great deal of advice, some helpful, some ridiculous, some based on myth and some reflecting truths. When Sue and I became parents, we received a simple, very meaningful present. It was a plaque entitled "To a Loving Parent" and it expressed the importance of spending time with your child and taking time for yourself. The plaque text reminds parents of the need for two-way communication, with an emphasis on listening. It stresses limiting negative feedback and providing limitless positive reinforcement for building a child's self-esteem. It extols planned activities and special spontaneous happenings. It emphasizes the significance of growing as individuals and as a family, of "being there" and also being aware of the needs and challenges of a growing child. It declares the critical role you will play in a child's life. Most of all, it portrays the joy and love of sharing the everyday special moments of your lives together.

"To a Loving Parent" was written by Rita Shaw in 1976 to provide inspiration for parents. When I spoke with Rita, she shared that even during the time when she was raising four children as a single parent, certain times together were extremely important. Rita noted, "One rule in particular was almost inflexible. We made it a point to gather around the dining table for dinner each evening and have an open forum. Everyone was allowed to say whatever he or she wished."

Rita realized that with "a few simple truths, raising a child could be rewarding and fun." Rita's experiences and insight are summarized in the words of "To a Loving Parent."[6]

"To a Loving Parent"

(Copyright 1980, Great Days Publishing, Santa Barbara, CA)

When the baby cries and you are tired, know that this time will pass, and when your child leaves for kindergarten you will have forgotten the difficult times.

Find, if you can, a few minutes each day just for you. Close your eyes. Be still. Rest. You deserve it.

Try to listen. Listen to the thoughts, the dreams, the anxieties and laughter your child wants to share with you.

Praise your child. Say "Wonderful!" "Thank you" and "Please." Say "I love you" and "What a good idea." Don't say "No" when you can say "Yes." Help your child become a comfortable individual.

Don't say cruel or hurtful things when you are tired or angry at something or someone else. Apologize to your children when you are wrong. Say "I'm sorry." It will teach them to do the same.

Each day find something loving and warm to say to your child and to yourself. Never beat a child. It only teaches that violence is acceptable behavior. Count to ten instead.

Find inexpensive things to do. A walk, a bus ride. Sit together, learn things together. Laugh together. Encourage your child to question, to be curious.

Share things about yourself. Let your children know you as a person, not as a parent who never makes mistakes. Let them see that you are an individual, too.

Introduce your child to books. Go to the library together. Read aloud together. Sing songs. Paint stones.

Try to set aside one mealtime each day when each of you—children and adults—can tell the family something that happened during the day. You will learn a lot from and about each other.

Let your child discover and learn independence by doing things alone and to make mistakes. Mistakes do not mean failure. We all make mistakes; it is a necessary learning process. Let your child help in small ways. Bed-making, dishes, setting the table, feeding pets. Don't set your standards too high.

Remind yourself that in a few short years your little one will be grown and gone—to a life of his or her own. Treasure the time you have together. Write down the funny things your child says and does. They will provide you with precious memories.

Be open to change and accept it. Change is inevitable. Remember that each day is a new beginning.

As best you can, help your children to grow up as happy individuals. It is a priceless legacy, one that will enable them to achieve adulthood knowing they are worthwhile and that life is good.

Generations of Memories

The date is marked in bright red on our calendar in the kitchen. This Sunday is "the day." Our family is taking a day trip to the West Point Military Academy, with a full afternoon of activities planned. The schedule we've been planning together for the last two weeks includes a tour of the museum, viewing the cadet parade, a leisurely walk on the magnificent grounds, lunch, and finally the enjoyment of listening to the West Point band in the outdoor amphitheater. We've already started to get together some of the things we need, such as blankets, a cooler, cameras and a pair of binoculars.

It's a trip that Ryan and Zachary are looking forward to, as it will be their first visit to a place we've talked about at length. But it is I who will truly cherish this day. Why? It will be a day that brings together three generations of memories. It's probably been more than eleven years now since Sue and I organized a trip for some thirty boys, grades 4 to 6, and their fathers while I was working at the YMCA in Connecticut. We attended a West Point football game. I forget the team West Point was playing, or even who won, but I still remember the cold, damp weather of that November day. The parents and children remember it, too, and laugh about how much hot chocolate and coffee everyone drank.

That day had special meaning, but more significant for me are previous visits I've made to West Point more than twenty-five years ago. My parents took our family to West Point for trips similar to the one we had planned for this Sunday. As a child, I clearly remember the parades, the huge cannons that were displayed on the grounds and, of course, the Sunday-evening summer concerts. We always arrived early to reserve a good spot on the lawn with our blankets, giving us plenty of time to climb on the cannons, as well as an early start on the snacks we brought. Sue also grew up in this area, and she has similar memories of visiting West Point.

I know this Sunday will be an exciting day for Ryan and Zachary—and also for Sue and me—but more importantly, it will be a memorable time for us, sharing a special time together as a family. It is very clear to me that family life during a child's early years is of the utmost importance. Your child wants to be with you and needs to be with you. Don't disappoint him or her and don't miss out yourself. The very special opportunity of being with your youngster only comes once. Start today.

S T A R T IS: SHAPING TOMORROW'S ADULTS BY REACHING OUT TODAY

DAY 31 : START today to give your undivided attention and unconditional love to your child. Saying "I'll do it tomorrow" just might be too late!

"I Forgot to Give Her a Hug."

From September 16-21, 1989, Hurricane Hugo caused destruction in the Caribbean and in South Carolina, followed soon after by an earthquake in San Francisco on October 17, 1989. These disasters caused significant structural damage, but more important was the loss of human life. From the media coverage we got a fairly accurate assessment of the physical damage, but not of the feelings and emotions of shock and devastation by those who lost their loved ones.

The Northeast is not known for severe storms or earthquakes—at least it wasn't before November 16, 1989. That day strong winds and rains struck the New York area where my family lives, ripping shutters off houses and uprooting trees. Ten miles from my home, tragedy struck. With winds over 90 miles per hour, a tornado hit the East Coldenham Elementary School, killing nine children and seriously injuring ten more. A catastrophe of this magnitude strongly affects an entire community. Teachers, fire-fighters, nurses, doctors, and especially parents felt the horrible effects of this tragedy. It was yet another time for a community and the nation as a whole to reflect on the importance and fragility of life, especially a child's life. As New York Governor Mario M. Cuomo said of these children, "So young, so bright, so innocent, so loved and so lovely."

John Lichtler, father of seven-year-old Joanna, whose life was lost when the school cafeteria wall collapsed, recounts the morning of November 16. "I put her on the bus that morning, like I do every morning. I kissed her good-bye, but I forgot to give her a hug."

As a parent, you must realize that every moment of life is special. Take the time and spend it with your child now for it will truly be quantity time well spent.

"The best inheritance you can give your children is a little time each day."

—*Anonymous*

9

A Twelve-Month Guide to Spending More Time with Your Child

As a parent, your days may become unbearably stressful. Nights may become long and tiring. As a treat to yourself (and your children) rent *Hook,* the Steven Spielberg film. The movie is an enjoyable show for the entire family, but it is also a reminder on the importance of spending time with your child. In the movie, actor Robin Williams plays a middle-aged lawyer named Peter Banning (who is also Peter Pan). Peter Banning is a very successful lawyer who can't seem to find enough time for his children. This is demonstrated very vividly by Peter missing his son's special baseball game, a game Peter promised he would make.

A few days later while the family is in England, Peter takes an overseas call relating to his work and suddenly gets very angry at his children for talking loudly. After this outburst and the children are asked to leave the room, Peter's wife shares some very sound insight with Peter. She tells him:

> **"Your children love you. They want to play with you. How long do you think that lasts? Soon Jack may not even want you to come to his games! We have a few special years with our children when**

they're the ones that want us around. After that
you are going to be running after them for a bit of
attention.

It goes so fast, Peter.
It's a few years. And then it's over.
And you are not being careful.
And you are missing it!"[1]

The following section will help you make time for those special
baseball games and other important events in your child's life. Make
sure you take advantage of this helpful guide.

You'll find thirty-one START principles along with the day of the
month(s) they are designed for. Use this setup for just one month, any
number of months or, best yet, for a full year. This section is very important in making an effort to improve your relationship with your child.
It is not just another exercise to keep you busy every day. Instead it is
an activity that empowers you! It empowers you to improve your relationship with your child, and it will help your child grow as an individual and as a caring member of the family.

Read each START principle in the morning and think of how you
will apply this principle with your child(ren) sometime during the day
or evening (even if it's just a phone call). Reread the START principle
during the day and once more during the evening. Record how you
put that START principle into action. This "START Log" is a process
that literally takes minutes, but it will have a major positive impact
on your relationship with your child.

The following list will serve as a reference for finding the section
of this book that each START principle is elaborated on. Use this
handy reference to refamiliarize yourself with the details of each START
principle:

START Principle for: **Refer to Information on Page:**

START LOG

START is your active involvement with children
DAY 1 OF EACH MONTH

START appreciating the beauty and remarkable development of
your child.
BECAUSE it stimulates a new and refreshing view of life and the
world around us.

DATE	YOUR APPLICATION OF TODAY'S FOCUS
JANUARY 1	
FEBRUARY 1	
MARCH 1	
APRIL 1	
MAY 1	
JUNE 1	
JULY 1	
AUGUST 1	
SEPTEMBER 1	
OCTOBER 1	
NOVEMBER 1	
DECEMBER 1	

START LOG

START is your active involvement with children
DAY 2 OF EACH MONTH

START being a major factor in building your child's personality,
intelligence, and self-esteem.
BECAUSE the sharing of your knowledge and love produces a
strong foundation for your child.

DATE	YOUR APPLICATION OF TODAY'S FOCUS
JANUARY 2	_____
FEBRUARY 2	_____
MARCH 2	_____
APRIL 2	_____
MAY 2	_____
JUNE 2	_____
JULY 2	_____
AUGUST 2	_____
SEPTEMBER 2	_____
OCTOBER 2	_____
NOVEMBER 2	_____
DECEMBER 2	_____

START LOG

START is your active involvement with children
DAY 3 OF EACH MONTH

START understanding your role as a parent and its effect on your
child, yourself, and those around you.
BECAUSE this generates the needed appreciation, sensitivity,
understanding, and insight in your new capacity

DATE	YOUR APPLICATION OF TODAY'S FOCUS
JANUARY 3	
FEBRUARY 3	
MARCH 3	
APRIL 3	
MAY 3	
JUNE 3	
JULY 3	
AUGUST 3	
SEPTEMBER 3	
OCTOBER 3	
NOVEMBER 3	
DECEMBER 3	

START LOG

START is your active involvement with children
DAY 4 OF EACH MONTH

START engaging in life's adventures with your children.
BECAUSE this is the first step to an enriching, lifelong relationship.

DATE	YOUR APPLICATION OF TODAY'S FOCUS
JANUARY 4	
FEBRUARY 4	
MARCH 4	
APRIL 4	
MAY 4	
JUNE 4	
JULY 4	
AUGUST 4	
SEPTEMBER 4	
OCTOBER 4	
NOVEMBER 4	
DECEMBER 4	

A Twelve-Month Guide to Spending More Time with Your Child   **177**

START LOG

START IS: SHAPING TOMORROW'S ADULTS BY REACHING OUT TODAY

START is your active involvement with children
DAY 5 OF EACH MONTH

START providing your child's needs with enthusiasm and a positive attitude.
BECAUSE the enjoyable time you spend with your child improves your child's outlook on life and your view of your role as parent.

DATE	YOUR APPLICATION OF TODAY'S FOCUS
JANUARY 5	
FEBRUARY 5	
MARCH 5	
APRIL 5	
MAY 5	
JUNE 5	
JULY 5	
AUGUST 5	
SEPTEMBER 5	
OCTOBER 5	
NOVEMBER 5	
DECEMBER 5	

START LOG

START is your active involvement with children
DAY 6 OF EACH MONTH

START "giving up" some of your personal time for your family. BECAUSE "sacrifices" produce winning teams (families) and a better functioning society.

DATE	YOUR APPLICATION OF TODAY'S FOCUS
JANUARY 6	
FEBRUARY 6	
MARCH 6	
APRIL 6	
MAY 6	
JUNE 6	
JULY 6	
AUGUST 6	
SEPTEMBER 6	
OCTOBER 6	
NOVEMBER 6	
DECEMBER 6	

START LOG

START is your active involvement with children
DAY 7 OF EACH MONTH

> START realizing that if you give your child your undivided attention, you will both enjoy the time together.
> BECAUSE spending time together will give you and your child many satisfying and gratifying experiences.

DATE	YOUR APPLICATION OF TODAY'S FOCUS
JANUARY 7	
FEBRUARY 7	
MARCH 7	
APRIL 7	
MAY 7	
JUNE 7	
JULY 7	
AUGUST 7	
SEPTEMBER 7	
OCTOBER 7	
NOVEMBER 7	
DECEMBER 7	

START LOG

START IS YOUR ACTIVE INVOLVEMENT WITH CHILDREN
DAY 8 OF EACH MONTH

START striving for active participation and open communication with your child.
BECAUSE you will develop a close personal tie with child as a result.

DATE	YOUR APPLICATION OF TODAY'S FOCUS
JANUARY 8	
FEBRUARY 8	
MARCH 8	
APRIL 8	
MAY 8	
JUNE 8	
JULY 8	
AUGUST 8	
SEPTEMBER 8	
OCTOBER 8	
NOVEMBER 8	
DECEMBER 8	

START LOG

START is your active involvement with children
DAY 9 OF EACH MONTH

START designating time with your child and family as a high priority.
BECAUSE making this investiment today brings tomorrow's dividends.

DATE	YOUR APPLICATION OF TODAY'S FOCUS
JANUARY 9	
FEBRUARY 9	
MARCH 9	
APRIL 9	
MAY 9	
JUNE 9	
JULY 9	
AUGUST 9	
SEPTEMBER 9	
OCTOBER 9	
NOVEMBER 9	
DECEMBER 9	

START LOG

START is your active involvement with children
DAY 10 OF EACH MONTH

> START "making today count" and develop a lasting and fulfilling relationship with your family.
> BECAUSE this will alleviate much stress, frustration, confusion, and guilt in the future.

DATE	YOUR APPLICATION OF TODAY'S FOCUS
JANUARY 10	
FEBRUARY 10	
MARCH 10	
APRIL 10	
MAY 10	
JUNE 10	
JULY 10	
AUGUST 10	
SEPTEMBER 10	
OCTOBER 10	
NOVEMBER 10	
DECEMBER 10	

START LOG

START IS: SHAPING TOMORROW'S ADULTS BY REACHING OUT TODAY

START is your active involvement with children
DAY 11 OF EACH MONTH

START setting short- and long-term goals.
BECAUSE this will allow you to make the kinds of adjustments
and commitments you need to make to spend more time with
your child.

DATE	YOUR APPLICATION OF TODAY'S FOCUS
JANUARY 11	
FEBRUARY 11	
MARCH 11	
APRIL 11	
MAY 11	
JUNE 11	
JULY 11	
AUGUST 11	
SEPTEMBER 11	
OCTOBER 11	
NOVEMBER 11	
DECEMBER 11	

START LOG

START is your active involvement with children
DAY 12 OF EACH MONTH

START reorganizing your daily schedule by utilizing "time-savers" and controlling "time-wasters" to accommodate the time you want to spend with your family.
BECAUSE this will alleviate much stress, frustration, confusion, and guilt in the future.

DATE	YOUR APPLICATION OF TODAY'S FOCUS
JANUARY 12	
FEBRUARY 12	
MARCH 12	
APRIL 12	
MAY 12	
JUNE 12	
JULY 12	
AUGUST 12	
SEPTEMBER 12	
OCTOBER 12	
NOVEMBER 12	
DECEMBER 12	

START LOG

START IS: SHAPING TOMORROW'S ADULTS BY REACHING OUT TODAY

START is your active involvement with children
DAY 13 OF EACH MONTH

START acting as a positive catalyst for your child by providing an atmosphere of playfulness in your home.
BECAUSE this promotes enjoyment and growth in your child and closeness between the two of you.

DATE	YOUR APPLICATION OF TODAY'S FOCUS
JANUARY 13	
FEBRUARY 13	
MARCH 13	
APRIL 13	
MAY 13	
JUNE 13	
JULY 13	
AUGUST 13	
SEPTEMBER 13	
OCTOBER 13	
NOVEMBER 13	
DECEMBER 13	

START LOG

START is your active involvement with children
DAY 14 OF EACH MONTH

> **START** introducing your child to various activities from the "Six Activity Groups."
> BECAUSE this generates a well-balanced menu of interests and options.

DATE	YOUR APPLICATION OF TODAY'S FOCUS
JANUARY 14	
FEBRUARY 14	
MARCH 14	
APRIL 14	
MAY 14	
JUNE 14	
JULY 14	
AUGUST 14	
SEPTEMBER 14	
OCTOBER 14	
NOVEMBER 14	
DECEMBER 14	

START LOG

START is your active involvement with children
DAY 15 OF EACH MONTH

START making your child's environment stimulating, interesting,
stable, enjoyable, and safe.
BECAUSE a positive environment provides the right setting for
your child's inherited characteristics to develop to the fullest.

DATE	YOUR APPLICATION OF TODAY'S FOCUS
JANUARY 15	
FEBRUARY 15	
MARCH 15	
APRIL 15	
MAY 15	
JUNE 15	
JULY 15	
AUGUST 15	
SEPTEMBER 15	
OCTOBER 15	
NOVEMBER 15	
DECEMBER 15	

START LOG

START is your active involvement with children
DAY 16 OF EACH MONTH

START to be aware of your child's desire for freeplay, instruction and team play, each in varying amounts.
BECAUSE the integration of these options contributes to your child's individuality and prepares him or her for life and its many

DATE	YOUR APPLICATION OF TODAY'S FOCUS
JANUARY 16	
FEBRUARY 16	
MARCH 16	
APRIL 16	
MAY 16	
JUNE 16	
JULY 16	
AUGUST 16	
SEPTEMBER 16	
OCTOBER 16	
NOVEMBER 16	
DECEMBER 16	

START LOG

START is your active involvement with children
DAY 17 OF EACH MONTH

START planning and carrying out spontaneous activities with your child.
BECAUSE these everyday episodes will turn into special lifetime memories.

DATE	YOUR APPLICATION OF TODAY'S FOCUS
JANUARY 17	
FEBRUARY 17	
MARCH 17	
APRIL 17	
MAY 17	
JUNE 17	
JULY 17	
AUGUST 17	
SEPTEMBER 17	
OCTOBER 17	
NOVEMBER 17	
DECEMBER 17	

START LOG

START is your active involvement with children
DAY 18 OF EACH MONTH

START to create the Three R's—routines, rituals, and the ridiculous in your child's life.
BECAUSE these are the seeds that transform everyday events into childhood "unforgettables."

DATE	YOUR APPLICATION OF TODAY'S FOCUS
JANUARY 18	_____
FEBRUARY 18	_____
MARCH 18	_____
APRIL 18	_____
MAY 18	_____
JUNE 18	_____
JULY 18	_____
AUGUST 18	_____
SEPTEMBER 18	_____
OCTOBER 18	_____
NOVEMBER 18	_____
DECEMBER 18	_____

START LOG

START is your active involvement with children
DAY 19 OF EACH MONTH

START helping your child build a good foundation for a lifetime of meaningful, fun activities.
BECAUSE this will expand your child's "free time" options and generate interests you can both share.

DATE	YOUR APPLICATION OF TODAY'S FOCUS
JANUARY 19	
FEBRUARY 19	
MARCH 19	
APRIL 19	
MAY 19	
JUNE 19	
JULY 19	
AUGUST 19	
SEPTEMBER 19	
OCTOBER 19	
NOVEMBER 19	
DECEMBER 19	

START LOG

START is your active involvement with children
DAY 20 OF EACH MONTH

START celebrating holidays and vacations in both "traditional"
ways and in your own distinct family manner.
BECAUSE the new events and customs you develop will become
enjoyable family traditions.

DATE	YOUR APPLICATION OF TODAY'S FOCUS
JANUARY 20	
FEBRUARY 20	
MARCH 20	
APRIL 20	
MAY 20	
JUNE 20	
JULY 20	
AUGUST 20	
SEPTEMBER 20	
OCTOBER 20	
NOVEMBER 20	
DECEMBER 20	

START LOG

START IS: SHAPING TOMORROW'S ADULTS BY REACHING OUT TODAY

START is your active involvement with children
DAY 21 OF EACH MONTH

START becoming alert to "those days" when you need rest.
BECAUSE being aware of this need is the first step to recovering
your balance, wellness, and happiness.

DATE   **YOUR APPLICATION OF TODAY'S FOCUS**

JANUARY 21   _____

FEBRUARY 21   _____

MARCH 21   _____

APRIL 21   _____

MAY 21   _____

JUNE 21   _____

JULY 21   _____

AUGUST 21   _____

SEPTEMBER 21   _____

OCTOBER 21   _____

NOVEMBER 21   _____

DECEMBER 21   _____

START LOG

START is your active involvement with children
DAY 22 OF EACH MONTH

START contacting helping agencies and services, including support groups, when the need arises.
BECAUSE these resources will assist you in overcoming the rough times in parenting.

DATE	YOUR APPLICATION OF TODAY'S FOCUS
JANUARY 22	
FEBRUARY 22	
MARCH 22	
APRIL 22	
MAY 22	
JUNE 22	
JULY 22	
AUGUST 22	
SEPTEMBER 22	
OCTOBER 22	
NOVEMBER 22	
DECEMBER 22	

START LOG

START is your active involvement with children
DAY 23 OF EACH MONTH

START scheduling some time for yourself by participating in one of your favorite activities.
BECAUSE you will become refreshed and rejuvenated.

DATE	YOUR APPLICATION OF TODAY'S FOCUS
JANUARY 23	
FEBRUARY 23	
MARCH 23	
APRIL 23	
MAY 23	
JUNE 23	
JULY 23	
AUGUST 23	
SEPTEMBER 23	
OCTOBER 23	
NOVEMBER 23	
DECEMBER 23	

START LOG

START IS: SHAPING TOMORROW'S ADULTS BY REACHING OUT TODAY

START is your active involvement with children
DAY 24 OF EACH MONTH

> START observing and evaluating the environment and people
> you leave your child with.
> BECAUSE proper surroundings will give your child valuable learn-
> ing experiences, and you will have greater peace of mind.

DATE	YOUR APPLICATION OF TODAY'S FOCUS
JANUARY 24	_____
FEBRUARY 24	_____
MARCH 24	_____
APRIL 24	_____
MAY 24	_____
JUNE 24	_____
JULY 24	_____
AUGUST 24	_____
SEPTEMBER 24	_____
OCTOBER 24	_____
NOVEMBER 24	_____
DECEMBER 24	_____

START LOG

START is your active involvement with children
DAY 25 OF EACH MONTH

START paying more attention to what you *do* than to what your preach.
BECAUSE children learn more by following examples than by verbal instructions.

DATE	YOUR APPLICATION OF TODAY'S FOCUS
JANUARY 25	
FEBRUARY 25	
MARCH 25	
APRIL 25	
MAY 25	
JUNE 25	
JULY 25	
AUGUST 25	
SEPTEMBER 25	
OCTOBER 25	
NOVEMBER 25	
DECEMBER 25	

START LOG

START is your active involvement with children
DAY 26 OF EACH MONTH

> **START** treating your child as you would life to be treated—the
> Golden Rule is alive and well!
> BECAUSE if your actions reflect this attitude, you will foster mutu-
> al consideration and respect.

DATE	YOUR APPLICATION OF TODAY'S FOCUS
JANUARY 26	
FEBRUARY 26	
MARCH 26	
APRIL 26	
MAY 26	
JUNE 26	
JULY 26	
AUGUST 26	
SEPTEMBER 26	
OCTOBER 26	
NOVEMBER 26	
DECEMBER 26	

START LOG

START is your active involvement with children
DAY 27 OF EACH MONTH

> START "being there" for your growing child. Provide the support
> and challenges to fulfill your child's changing needs and interests.
> BECAUSE your genuine interest . . .and quantity time . . .creates a
> trusting and lasting relationship.

DATE	YOUR APPLICATION OF TODAY'S FOCUS
JANUARY 27	
FEBRUARY 27	
MARCH 27	
APRIL 27	
MAY 27	
JUNE 27	
JULY 27	
AUGUST 27	
SEPTEMBER 27	
OCTOBER 27	
NOVEMBER 27	
DECEMBER 27	

START LOG

START IS: SHAPING TOMORROW'S ADULTS BY REACHING OUT TODAY

START is your active involvement with children
DAY 28 OF EACH MONTH

> START strengthening the traits needed for raising your child,
> including patience, understanding, flexibility, trust and, especial-
> ly, love.
> BECAUSE cultivating these traits will improve all your relationships.

DATE	YOUR APPLICATION OF TODAY'S FOCUS
JANUARY 28	_____
FEBRUARY 28	_____
MARCH 28	_____
APRIL 28	_____
MAY 28	_____
JUNE 28	_____
JULY 28	_____
AUGUST 28	_____
SEPTEMBER 28	_____
OCTOBER 28	_____
NOVEMBER 28	_____
DECEMBER 28	_____

START LOG

START is your active involvement with children
DAY 29 OF EACH MONTH

START taking care of finding the right balance in your life for work, family, and leisure.
BECAUSE harmony is the principal factor in achieving success.

DATE	YOUR APPLICATION OF TODAY'S FOCUS
JANUARY 29	
FEBRUARY 29	
MARCH 29	
APRIL 29	
MAY 29	
JUNE 29	
JULY 29	
AUGUST 29	
SEPTEMBER 29	
OCTOBER 29	
NOVEMBER 29	
DECEMBER 29	

START LOG

START is your active involvement with children
DAY 30 OF EACH MONTH

START being a loving parent, grandparent, teacher, child care worker, neighbor, or friend by spending time with a child. BECAUSE two people will be better for the effort—you and the child. The future of our children depends on you spending quantity time with them!

DATE	YOUR APPLICATION OF TODAY'S FOCUS
JANUARY 30	_____
FEBRUARY 30	_____
MARCH 30	_____
APRIL 30	_____
MAY 30	_____
JUNE 30	_____
JULY 30	_____
AUGUST 30	_____
SEPTEMBER 30	_____
OCTOBER 30	_____
NOVEMBER 30	_____
DECEMBER 30	_____

START LOG

S T A R T IS: SHAPING TOMORROW'S ADULTS BY REACHING OUT TODAY

START is your active involvement with children
DAY 31 OF EACH MONTH

> START today to give your undivided attention and unconditional love to your child.
> BECAUSE saying "I'll do it tomorrow" just might be too late!

DATE	YOUR APPLICATION OF TODAY'S FOCUS
JANUARY 31	
FEBRUARY 31	
MARCH 31	
APRIL 31	
MAY 31	
JUNE 31	
JULY 31	
AUGUST 31	
SEPTEMBER 31	
OCTOBER 31	
NOVEMBER 31	
DECEMBER 31	

Final Note

Let me share one more scene from the movie *Hook*. The scene revolves around Robin Williams going back to Never-Never Land to rescue his children, who were taken by Captain Hook. Captain James Hook puts the children in a net and hoists them up very high on his ship's mast in an attempt to get Peter Pan to fly. Robin Williams does not realize he has the power to fly; he climbs the mast to rescue his children. He tries very hard to rescue them but cannot reach them. His son, who earlier was very angry with his father for missing his baseball game, says very earnestly, "Please don't give up."

I am telling you, parent to parent, don't give up on your child and your family.

Don't ever give up.

More Than a Book

Author Steffen T. Kraehmer also conducts parenting and family related seminars and workshops. Programs with specific topics are suitable for schools, churches, and child care centers.

For seminar and workshop information, write to:

TWS Resources
Box 492
Plattekill, New York 12568-0492

Notes

CHAPTER 1

1. Roberts Rugh and Landrum B. Shettles, *From Conception to Birth*, New York: Harper and Row, 1971, p. 17.

2. Eric Fellman, *Daily Guideposts*, 1988, Carmel, New York: Guideposts, 1987, p. 109.

3. Benjamin S. Bloom, *All Our Children Learning: A Primer for Parents, Teachers and Other Educators*, New York: McGraw-Hill, 1981, pp. 72-73.

4. William Mitchell, *The Power of Positive Students*, New York: Bantam Books, 1985, p. 57-58.

5. J. L. McIntosh, *Suicide Data Page: 1986*, Washington, D.C.: U.S. Department of Health and Human Services Update, Public Health Service, 1988, p. 3.

6. Linda Ching Sledge, *Daily Guideposts*, 1990, Carmel, New York: Guideposts, 1989, pp. 86-87

CHAPTER 2

1. Bill Cosby, *Bill Cosby, Himself*, CBS Fox Video, 1988.

2. "The 'Quality Time' Myth," *Time Talk: The International Time Management and Productivity Newsletter*, September, 1986, Vol 9, No. 9, p. 1.

3. *What Works: Research about Teaching and Learning, Second Edition*, Washington, D.C.: U. S. Department of Education, GPO, 1987, p. 5.

4. Ann Landers, "Make Time for the Kids," *The Times Herald Record*, (Middletown, New York), June 2, 1988, p. 38, col. 1.

CHAPTER 3

1. Diane Booher, *Cutting Paperwork in a Corporate Culture*, New York: Facts on File Publications, New York, 1986, pp. 3-23.

2. Ibid.

3. Ibid.

4, "Executive Style Survey", *The Wall Street Journal*, March 20, 1987, p. 21D.

CHAPTER 4

1. Cosby S. Rogers and Janet K. Sawyers, *Play in the Lives of Children*, Washington, D.C.: National Association for the Education of Young Children, 1988, p. 9.

2. Sue Spayth Riley, *How to Generate Values in Young Children*, Washington, D.C.: National Association for the Education of Young Children, 1984, p. 24.

3. Rogers and Sawyers, p. 9.

4. Ibid., p. 11.

5. *Product Safety Fact Sheet*, Washington, D.C.: U.S. Consumer Product Safety Commission, GPO, 1987, pp. 1-3.

6. "The Reading Report Card: Progress toward Excellence in Our Schools," *Eric Reports*, Washington, D.C.: U.S. Department of Education, 1985, p. 9.

7. Susan Ruotsala Storm, "Children's Learning from Broadcast Television: The Relationship Between the Amount of Time a Child Watches Television with and without Adults and That Child's Learning from Television," *Eric Reports*, Washington, D.C.: U.S. Department of Education, 1985, p. 1.

8. Ibid., pp. 8-9.

9. "The Reading Report Card," p.1.

10. *What Works: Research about Teaching and Learning, Second Edition*, Washington, D.C.: U.S. Department of Education, GPO, 1987, p. 7.

11. Ibid., p. 8.

12. Ibid., p. 23.

13. *Youth Fitness Fact Sheet*, Washington, D.C.: The President's Council on Physical Fitness and Sports, 1988, p. 1.

14. William Mitchell, *The Power of Positive Students*, New York: Bantam Books, 1985, pp. 165-66.

CHAPTER 5

1. Janet Martin, *Daily Guideposts, 1981*, Carmel, New York: Guideposts, 1987, pp. 170-171.

2. Monica E. Breidenbach and Margot K. Hover, *Christian Family Almanac*, Dubuque, Iowa: William C. Brown Company Publishers, Religious Education Division, 1980, p. 87.

3. Carol Knapp, Daily Guideposts, 1988, Carmel, New York: Guideposts, 1987, p. 143.

CHAPTER 6

1. J. Ingram Walker, M.D., "Stress", *The Encyclopedia Americana*, Danbury, Connecticut: Grolier, 1985, p. 794.

2. Thomas H. Holmes and Richard H. Rahe, "The Social Readjustment Rating Scale", *Journal of Psychosomatic Research*, Volume 11, pp. 213-218.

3. "Position Statement on Quality Child Care," Little Rock, Arkansas: The Southern Association on Children Under Six, 1986, p. 1.

4. Ibid, pp. 1-8.

CHAPTER 7

1. Leonard Zunin and Natalie Zunin, *Contact: The First Four Minutes*, New York: Ballantine Books, 1972, p. 156.

2. William Mitchell, *The Power of Positive Students*, New York: Bantam Books, 1985, pp. 145.

3. Sue Spayth Riley, *How to Generate Values in Young Children*, Washington, D. C.: National Association for the Education of Young Children, 1984, p. 11.

4. *Webster's Third New International Dictionary*, Springfield, Massachusetts: G. & C. Merriam Company, 1976, p. 1340.

5. *The Book*, Carmel, New York: Guideposts, 1971, pp. 1160-1161.

CHAPTER 8

1. Christopher Phillips, "Every Child Has a Right to Love," *Parade Magazine*, December 5, 1988, pp. 4-6.

2. *Guideposts*, Carmel, New York: Guideposts, March, 1988, p. 44.

3. Jerrold K. Footlick, "What Happened to the Family?" *Newsweek*, Winter/Spring 1990, p. 18.

4. Edith Schaeffer, *What is a Family?*, Old Tappan, New Jersey: Fleming Revell, 1975, p. 255.

5. Sidney B. Simon, Leland W. Howe, and Howard Kirschenbaum, *Values Clarification*, New York: Hart Publishing Company, 1972, p. 326.

6. *To a Loving Parent*, Santa Barbara, California, Great Days Publishing, 1988.

CHAPTER 9

1. Steven Speilberg, *Hook*, Columbia TriStar Home Video, 1992.

Index

About the Author

STEFFEN T. KRAEHMER has developed the START (Shaping Tomorrow's Adult by Reaching Out Today) principles, as well as related seminars and workshops for parents, teachers, and care givers. He has also created FIND, the Family Information Network Database. The FIND service gives individuals a personalized listing of agencies and programs relating to particular family related interests or needs.

He is on the Board of Directors for the Family Resource Coalition of New York (FRCNY). The author earned a Bachelor's degree in Leisure Services and Studies from Florida State University. During the past fifteen years, he has worked with thousands of youths in all age groups and their parents in numerous professional recreational settings—with corporations, government programs, churches, scouting programs, YMCAs, private fitness clubs, and municipal services.

He is presently the Assistant Director of the Outreach Ministries Department at *Guideposts* magazine. Steffen and his wife, Sue, both come from families of five children.

They reside in the state of New York with their two sons, Ryan and Zachary.